EMMA SLADE EDMONDSON

MIXED

Explore and Celebrate Your Mixed Identity

Illustrations by Tasia Graham

First published 2026 by Rocket Fox,
an imprint of Pan Macmillan
The Smithson, 6 Briset Street, London EC1M 5NR
EU representative: Macmillan Publishers Ireland Ltd, 1st Floor,
The Liffey Trust Centre, 117–126 Sheriff Street Upper, Dublin 1 D01 YC43
Associated companies throughout the world

ISBN 978-1-0350-4161-9

Text copyright © Emma Slade Edmondson 2026
Illustrations copyright © Tasia Graham 2026

The right of Emma Slade Edmondson and Tasia Graham to be identified
as the author and illustrator of this work has been asserted
in accordance with the Copyright, Designs and Patents Act 1988.

All rights reserved. No part of this publication may be reproduced,
stored in a retrieval system, or transmitted, in any form, or by any means
(including, without limitation, electronic, mechanical, photocopying, recording
or otherwise) without the prior written permission of the publisher.

Pan Macmillan does not have any control over, or any responsibility for,
any author or third-party websites (including, without limitation, URLs,
emails and QR codes) referred to in or on this book.

1 3 5 7 9 8 6 4 2

A CIP catalogue record for this book is available from the British Library.

Printed and bound in the UK using 100% Renewable Electricity by CPI Group (UK) Ltd
Designed by Janene Spencer

This book is sold subject to the condition that it shall not, by way of trade or otherwise,
be lent, hired out, or otherwise circulated without the publisher's prior consent in any
form of binding or cover other than that in which it is published and without a similar
condition including this condition being imposed on the subsequent purchaser.
The publisher does not authorize the use or reproduction of any part of this book in
any manner for the purpose of training artificial intelligence technologies or systems.
The publisher expressly reserves this book from the Text and Data Mining exception in
accordance with Article 4(3) of the European Union Digital Single Market Directive 2019/790.

Visit **www.panmacmillan.com** to read more about all our books and to buy them.

To my northern grandparents, Granny Katy and Grandad Stephen, whose passion for teaching and inspiring young people, in turn, encouraged me to share what I've learnt with the next generation.

© Coomy Ogbewele

About the Author

Emma Slade Edmondson is a sustainability consultant, writer, journalist, podcaster, TEDx speaker and presenter. A change maker and leader in the sustainable fashion and retail space for over ten years.

She is the co-host of the award-winning podcast *Mixed Up*, which is a deep dive into race and identity from the mixed perspective. Guests have included Mel B, Big Zuu, Jordan Stephens, David Oyelowo, Anton Ferdinand, Candice Brathwaite, Travis Alabanza, Lianne La Havas and Ben Bailey Smith, to name a few.

She founded Good Form, a creative strategic marketing agency working to elevate brands, initiatives and organizations that are committed to a more sustainable future. She is recognized as a *Forbes* 100 environmentalist and is deeply interested in an intersectional approach to environmentalism.

CONTENTS

	About the Author	vi
	Dear Reader	1
1.	The Question	9
2.	Language Matters	35
3.	The Chat	69
4.	The History of the Mixed Experience	85
5.	Making Positive Connections	115
6.	Language and Belonging	155
7.	Identity Fluidity	171
8.	You Decide	187
	A Final Letter	205
	Glossary	208
	About the Illustrator	211
	Acknowledgements	212

Dear Reader,

I'm **Emma Slade Edmondson**, and I'm so happy to be writing to you.

I always find introductions a little difficult because (as I often say to other people when they ask me about myself) I wear a lot of hats. And by that, I mean I find it hard to describe exactly who I am and what I do clearly, and without too many words. But I'm going to give it a try – so here goes . . .

My name is Emma, and I am an author. I am **also** a podcaster, which means I get to chat to a lot of interesting people so that others can listen to our conversations.

Sometimes I'll interview people more formally, like you might see on TV or on the news, and other times we will just have more of a casual chat. But either way I **always, always** learn a lot from the people I talk to, especially when they have different life experiences from me. That's what I love most about making podcasts – it allows you to connect with others and to hear really rich and interesting stories about their lives.

I think that listening to other people's stories is a brilliant way to learn more about the world and the different people in it.

My podcast is called *Mixed Up* and – just like this book – it's all about the experience of being mixed-race. I am mixed. I was born in Britain, and my mum and her family are white British, originally from Cornwall, but I also have Jamaican heritage, and I am also part German Swiss.

I am **all** of these things **at once**.

My biological father's family is from Jamaica. The north of Jamaica specifically, and they are Afro Jamaicans.

I recently also learnt that part of my ancestry is Nigerian.

which makes a lot of sense because I LOVE jollof rice so much (honestly, I could scoff so many plates in one sitting, and always have to take a little packed lunch home in a container when I visit my mum-in-law).

I have a huge round Afro (which I almost always wear as brushed out as big as I can get it), and I have big brown eyes and brown skin. On the other hand, my brothers are white with blond-brown hair and my dad, who brought me up and has looked after me all my life, is white and northern. That means I am the only mixed-race person in my close family.

It has taken me some time to be comfortable with all of the things I am because I used to find that being mixed-race **can, not always**, but at some points in life, feel lonely – sometimes it might feel like you are the only one. But talking about being mixed with lots of different people, and especially people who are also of mixed heritage, has helped me HUGELY. It's helped me to understand how many mixed people there are in the world, and how we all have unique stories – stories that can bring us together.

HERITAGE:

The word 'heritage' brings together lots of special things that are relevant to your family's past — stories, traditions, values — which come from your family and their culture. Your heritage can help you feel connected to your living family and also past members of your family. Understanding your heritage can make you feel proud of where you come from. And discovering more about it can be really interesting!

Through my podcast, I have spoken to footballers, historians, nurses, actors and actresses, and even famous singers and chefs, like Mel B and Big Zuu.

We have shared stories. We've cried together, when talking about things that have been difficult for us, times when we've been misunderstood or hurt by feeling excluded by different groups. But we've also laughed together, discussing shared experiences.

It's been interesting to find out about how different it is growing up mixed in other countries outside of the UK. We'll talk more about the differences we experience because of geography, location and exactly where we all grow up later in the book . . . but for now I want to finish this letter by telling you about one of the most important things I've learnt through making my podcast – mixed-race people come in all different forms.

Quite often on TV or in the papers and magazines (especially in the UK) we are portrayed as having one Black parent and one white parent. But I've met people who are Japanese-Jamaican, people who are Filipino-Ghanaian, people who are Mexican-Italian and someone just recently who is Iranian-Venezuelan. We are all so different, but in some respects, there are many things that unify us, and I want to talk about both our differences and our similarities in this book.

Because our stories are unique, and there's no one way to be mixed, I've asked a few of my mixed-race friends to write letters that you'll see throughout the book. I have always loved letter writing and pen pals, so I thought this would be the perfect way we can all learn together, from experiences that are not our own. You might find that you can relate to the experiences of my friends, or that what they're saying prompts you to think about your own identity differently.

To tell you the truth, I've been on a bit of a journey with my identity. In fact, if I'm really honest with you, I am still on that journey. I believe that we may all be on a journey with our identities for our whole lives.

And that's OK.

It's actually a good thing because being willing to grow and learn about yourself is a really positive thing that can give you a real sense of pride. It can make you feel more aware and more confident to talk to other people about their own background and their cultures, which also helps us all be more considerate and understanding of one another.

I've had such a positive experience making the podcast, that I decided to write this book to share the things I learnt along the way. This book is one that I wish I'd had when I was younger. Having this information would have really helped me feel more confident and proud of myself. It would have answered questions I didn't quite know how to ask the friends and family around me.

I hope that this book inspires you to be bold in the discovery of who you are, how you want to describe yourself and put yourself out into the world. I want it to help you begin to answer questions that might feel difficult right now. Use what you read here about other people's experiences to support you in pushing back against the idea that you have to **choose** one side of your heritage over another, or that you need to be what other people say you are versus who you understand yourself to be.

I want to tell you that no matter where you may go or what you may hear, you are **complete** just as you are. You are **enough**. Not half of one thing and half of another, or more of one thing and too little of another simply because someone else says so (unless of course you decide that that is how you would like to describe yourself). In which case that's just fine.

Who you are is really up to you.

Emma Slade Edmondson x x

1
The Question

Dean Atta

is a British poet — his poetry often explores questions about identity and social justice.

Dear Reader,

Dean here, nice to meet you.

When I was ten, people often asked me where I was from. Sometimes, they wanted to know which part of London I was from, but usually, they wanted to know about my heritage.

> **My mum's family is from Cyprus, and my dad's family is from Jamaica.**

> **That's an interesting mix.**

It is an interesting mix. Later, I learnt that Cyprus and Jamaica were once part of the British Empire as colonies – both countries have a complicated history with the United Kingdom.

I didn't visit Cyprus until I was fifteen, and I didn't visit Jamaica until I was an adult. When I was ten, what I knew about Cyprus and Jamaica came from family, family friends, schoolteachers, and school friends, as well as what I watched on TV and heard on the radio.

I didn't have access to the internet back then, so I couldn't just look it up. But I could've gone to the library to borrow books about Cyprus and Jamaica, or I could've turned to the encyclopaedias my mum bought me. These big books, full of facts, started with the letter A and went to the letter Z. However, I didn't look in Book C for Cyprus or Book J for Jamaica because I'm dyslexic and found reading difficult back then. My identity felt as jumbled as words on the page, especially new words. And at ten, so many things were new to me. I often heard new words I didn't understand in the languages my family spoke

PATOIS:

Patois is a language spoken by Jamaicans that is a combination of English and West African languages.

around me – Cypriot Greek and Jamaican **Patois**. But my family in London could all speak English as well, so it wasn't until I visited Cyprus at fifteen and met family members who didn't speak English that I felt excluded from conversations.

If I could give one piece of advice to anyone with another language in their family, it would be to learn that language. It will help you connect with your family and others who share your heritage. It could make visiting a country of your heritage easier and more fulfilling. You may consider moving there for a period of your life.

If I could give a second piece of advice to all mixed people, it would be to ask your elders (older family members) about their lives. When I began to ask my grandparents, great-aunts and great-uncles about their lives, I found I understood my parents, aunts and uncles better, and in doing so,

I understood myself better.

Our elders are like the internet, or the encyclopaedias I described earlier. Full of information. But many won't share their wisdom with us unless we ask them. We may not always agree with our elders' opinions or follow the same customs and traditions, but it is worth trying to understand why our elders think and do what they do.

Here are some ideas of questions you could ask your elders:

- What was your life like at my age?
- Who raised you, and what were they like?
- Do you have any favourite memories?
- Will you teach me a recipe that's special to you?

I hope asking them these questions will help you feel closer to them and lead you to a deeper understanding of your family as a whole.

Food has always been my special connection to my family and heritage. I learnt to make egg-lemon soup the way my Cypriot grandmother made it, and rice and peas the way my Jamaican grandmother taught me. I've also taught myself to make other Cypriot and Jamaican dishes from recipe books and the internet.

I know not everyone has their elders around. When I haven't been able to get answers from elders, I've turned to books, films, TV shows and the internet to fill the gaps in my understanding. But I've realized *there's no such thing as a complete or total understanding of yourself or your heritage.*

And what you think of as fact is often more complicated than an encyclopaedia, elder or any book can explain.

Dean Atta x

> **'What are you?'**

OR > **'Where are you from?'**

is probably (I'm going to bet) a question you've been asked before.

It's certainly a question I've been asked many times, and when I talked to some of my friends and the awesome people who wrote the letters in this book, they all agreed that a version of this question is up there as one of the things they are asked most frequently.

But what does this question really mean? What information are people actually looking for when they ask this?

Well, this is interesting because it's what we call a loaded question. That means that although on the face of it's just one question, if you look a little closer it's actually loaded up with many questions layered on top of one another – a bit like a **question burger.**

For example, when people ask you **'Where are you from?'**, they could be asking what town or city you live in. They could be asking where you were born, they could be asking what country your parents were born in, or, they could be asking what race or ethnicity you are. Or like Dean mentioned in his letter, they could be asking about your heritage and where your parents and their parents were born (without explicitly asking).

QUICK DICTIONARY PULL-OUT

RACE

The idea of race as we know it today was created by European philosophers as a system to identify and group people across the world based on the way they look, whether it's their skin colour, hair texture, facial features or eye shape. This way of grouping people has been used as a way for people in one group to falsely claim that they are better than, and more deserving, than those in another group.

People are often grouped into categories of race like: Black, Asian, Mixed or White.

People who are **racialized** as Black or brown are often asked this whether or not they are mixed, but I think the reason people often ask this question of mixed people is because it really is human nature to want to label and sort things into groups and categories that feel easier to understand. Many people might at first find it difficult to place mixed-race people, because we don't look like the people they are already personally familiar with or because they are used to being able to decide who they think someone is just from how they look or sound.

QUICK DICTIONARY PULL-OUT

RACIALIZED

The way people categorize or divide people into groups according to their race. For example – I am mainly **racialized** by people as Black because they see visual cues like my Afro and my nose shape and my skin colour. I am actually mixed-race (Black Jamaican and white British), but because people tend to categorize me as Black based on what they see, I am most often 'racialized' by the world as Black.

In my experience, when people ask 'Where are you from?', they often hope you'll tell them about your ethnicity or heritage because this is one of the things they might use to try to understand the kind of person they think you are. Some people will be asking because they genuinely want to know more about you, but it might also make you feel uncomfortable – and if that's the case it's OK to not answer if you don't want to. It's also OK to not answer if you feel like you don't know the answer to the question.

Sometimes, if you respond to 'Where are you from?' by telling the person where you live or where you grew up, they might say, 'But where are you **really** from?'. This question makes me feel quite uncomfortable. I think it makes me feel like this because it feels a little like they are digging for something, or that they are not satisfied with the answer you've already given.

In my opinion, if this question makes you feel uneasy, it is OK to either:

1. Avoid answering it, or

2. Ask them a question in response.

So – instead of answering – you may want to respond with something like:

1. *I'm not sure what exactly you mean by that, because I just explained where I'm from. I'm a bit confused by your question.*

2. *I don't feel comfortable giving you more information about that at the moment.*

3. *Maybe you could tell me a little bit about yourself and where you're from first?*

It is human psychology to want to 'organize' things in our minds, and in our world, so that it's easier for us to think about and understand. And in fact, this is exactly where **stereotypes** come from (this is something we will talk more about a bit later).

QUICK DICTIONARY PULL-OUT

STEREOTYPE

A belief about a type of person or a group that is over simplified, not very thoughtful or considered, but nevertheless widely held and quite fixed in the minds of people.

Mixed-race people can be difficult to categorize because it doesn't feel as if we fit neatly into any of the boxes people are working with. Being mixed-race means that we don't have one **ethnicity**. Often, we may have a complex identity that combines two or more ethnicities or cultural backgrounds. Like Dean was explaining in his letter, we may have two or more different traditions, religious practices, languages, or even favourite foods that our parents or the elders in our family have shared with us. These cultures can be very different from one another because they come from parts of the world with very different traditions. And on top of that, mixed-race people might not look the way that someone might expect us to.

QUICK DICTIONARY PULL-OUT

ETHNICITY

A group of people who share the same heritage, background, traditions, customs and beliefs. Someone's ethnicity is different from their race, as it includes the society and culture a person belongs to. An ethnic group will have a shared history and a sense that they belong together.

The funny thing is that people often use the term 'ambiguous' to describe how they think mixed people look. This means they think our race is not easily identifiable: it's not immediately clear which race we belong to.

Personally, I don't like this term because it can sometimes feel quite dismissive and a bit negative, but I think it's a good way to illustrate how frustrated people can be when they don't know how to place you. They often feel they **need** a label.

> **The important thing to remember here is that only YOU are responsible for, and capable of, labelling your own identity. It is something that belongs to you.**

Most of the time this kind of questioning — asking things like 'Where are you from?' — comes from a curiosity about your identity that people have when they see you and it's tempting for them to start writing a story about this in their heads. But no matter how unsure you feel about where you fit in, as you are growing and learning about yourself (and maybe also your parents' heritage and histories), it really is up to you to define the answer to this question, whenever you're ready. Like Dean says in his letter, there may be a lot of questions you have around who you are, and your identity may feel 'jumbled' to you at the moment, but the good news is that there are lots of interesting ways to explore your identity — I hope this book can help you with that!

When I was younger I used to think a lot about how I didn't look that much like anyone in my family. Picture me – big Afro, brown skin, triangular nose shape and deep dark brown eyes. Now picture my mum, my two brothers and the man who has been a dad to me all my life – all white with blond-brown hair and blue eyes. I think you can imagine the questions running through other people's minds when they saw us out together as a family.

Now that I am older, I see that I do look a lot like my mum – although our skin colour is different, I have her smile, her chin and the exact same dimples on either side of my mouth when I smile. I also have a lot of her mannerisms. But when I was younger people often used to ask me if I was adopted. First they would ask 'Where are you from?' and then sometimes, 'What are you?' And, if they saw my parents, the question might become 'Are you adopted?' I remember that sometimes this made me feel embarrassed and even occasionally ashamed. I'm still not absolutely sure why I felt this way, but no one likes to be pointed out or picked as the odd one out in a group, and especially not in their own family. It can be embarrassing to be asked questions in a crowd while people watch, and that is sort of what this kind of questioning felt like to me. I wanted to get away from whoever was asking the question as quickly as possible or change the subject.

> **When people see our parents and then they can't quite do the calculation to work out our heritage, they often lurch to other explanations.**

If you have ever experienced something like this and found it upsetting or frustrating, I'm sorry. If so, you might like to do the talking activity below with your parents or even with a friend.

The activity over the page is designed to help you to practise talking about your identities and yourself. It should hopefully help you be firm with other people about who you are, and allow you to stand up for yourself – especially if you are uncomfortable when being asked questions like the ones I described above. With practice and repetition, this will eventually make you feel more confident.

EXERCISE NO.1

TALKING ABOUT OUR MIXED IDENTITIES

Try to answer the following questions on your own, and then find someone you feel comfortable with to try talking your answers through with them.

- **What words would you use to describe yourself, your race and your heritage?**

- **Do you think this is different from how your parents, family or friends would describe you? If so, how?**

- **How do those differences in your description and their description make you feel?**

- **It can be really difficult to hear someone describe you in a way that you're not comfortable with. How do you react if you hear someone describe you differently from the words you've used above?**

- **Do you feel more drawn to one side of your heritage than another?**

- **How do you see yourself? What words spring to mind when you think about the kind of person you are? Who are your role models? Who do you look up to? What inspires you to do the things you do? What foods do you like? Where do you feel most comfortable, and who with? How do you feel about the way you look?**

- **Do you think this is different from how others see you?**

- **Do you have any words that people have used to describe you that make you feel bad or negative about your identity? Why do you think this is?**

- **Notice what words you use to describe yourself. Why do these words feel right?**

QUICK DICTIONARY PULL-OUT

IDENTITY

How you see who you are and how you fit into the world. This can be based on lots of different things – including what you look like, how you are racialized, your gender, ethnicity, your religious faith, dis/ability, languages you speak, where you grew up in the world, or even where your parents were born.

What do you know about your heritage? For example, are there any foods, recipes, languages or stories you know? Are there things you don't know that you would like to? Grab a piece of paper and write out a list of them. (We will come back to these later when we get to 'The Chat'.)

Microaggressions and how to deal with them

Sometimes these actions or words might feel subtle, or they might be difficult to understand, but they will almost always make you feel bad.

The questions   **'What are you?'**

and   'Where are you from?'

are considered to be microaggressions, but another example might be someone suggesting that your hair looks better when it is straightened as opposed to when it's curly or in an Afro. The reason this is a negative and unfriendly comment is because it comes from the idea that straighter hair looks better than Afro or curly hair. This is a European and white beauty standard, which has been reinforced to us through books and art throughout recent history. Because straight hair is more commonly found on white people, and of course none of us can change the way our hair grows out of our head, it's a way of making a racist comment that may make you feel 'less than'. It is not necessarily always super obvious, but it does come from a racist idea.

Thankfully, people are becoming more and more aware that making these kinds of comments to schoolmates or family, or even friends, is inappropriate. But there is still work to be done –

I want to empower you to help others get better at recognizing how their comments and conversations might make you feel.

You can do that simply by practising expressing yourself aloud – describing yourself however you feel comfortable so people can follow your lead.

QUICK DICTIONARY PULL-OUT

MICROAGGRESSION

Microaggression is a term for commonly used language or behaviour that can be intentionally or unintentionally unfriendly or negative in its attitudes towards groups who are already being treated as less important than others by society. We call this marginalization.

Examples of groups that are often marginalized might be:

1. Disabled people
2. People who are not white
3. People from the LGBTQIA+ community

There are many more examples but these are three good examples to help you understand this term.

Overt aggressions/ macroaggressions and overt racism

One of my friends, Becca Dudley, who is a reggae DJ, recently told me that because she is very fair-skinned, she often has to explain that she is mixed-race and that her grandad is from Annotto Bay in Jamaica. One day when she was explaining this, she was aggressively told by someone that 'I don't care what you say' because 'you are not mixed, you are a white girl'.

This response to her talking about her identity can be described as a 'macroaggression' or a more overt racism. This is because the person is directly denying or arguing with Becca's identity and heritage even though she's already been clear about her grandad.

2

Language Matters

Tori Tsui

is a Hong Kong-born environmental campaigner, award-winning author, and advisor based in England, fighting for a greener future.

Dear Reader,

My name is Tori Tsui,

When I was younger, I used to believe that I was divisible; that my identity could be broken down into lots of different pieces. After all, my mum was born in Hong Kong and my dad was born in England. She was Chinese and he was English. I'm 50% this and 50% that.

However, thinking this way made me feel alien and like I didn't belong. It meant I never quite fit in with people who were 100% English or 100% Chinese. I wasn't 'enough' of either and I never quite felt at home around people who belonged exclusively to one group. I could relate to people over some things, but not everything.

Over the years I've come to appreciate that I'm 100% me. I've learnt that I am whole and enough as I am. These days I call myself Eurasian – which means I have a mix of European and Asian parentage – because it feels like a term that fits for me, one that allows me to be proud of my mixed-race identity and one that honours my dual heritage. And through this I've come to celebrate the beautiful ways in which these two cultures collide and mix together. I no longer see them as separate and I no longer believe that I'm half of anything. I am wholly human as I am.

Sure, I might not fully 'fit' into any one culture. But what's beautiful is that I fully relate to everyone who finds the experience of relating really tough. I find comfort in talking to other mixed-race people or even people who have moved from their home countries to a new one. There is so much belonging in the feeling of not belonging at all. And it is a unique experience that allows us to celebrate just how lucky we are to have grown up with these unique life experiences.

So here's to us, being fully ourselves, 100%.

Lots of love, Tori

It's really important to be thoughtful about the language we use,

particularly when we are talking about other people. The words we choose give them an idea about how we feel about them – even when we don't mean anything bad. If someone says something about someone else's skin colour or uses the term 'mixed' in a careless or unkind way, it might hurt their feelings or make them feel like they don't belong.

> ***Using thoughtful language helps us show respect and kindness.***

It says, 'I notice who you are, and every part of you is important to me'. When we use thoughtful language, we show others how to do the same, which helps make everyone feel welcome and safe, regardless of where their family comes from.

The language and the labels we use to describe things tend to change over time, and often quite drastically as the years pass.

This is very much true of the words we use now to describe mixed-race people and experiences. Some of the things that your grandparents or the older people in your life might have told you they used to say when they were younger – and that they felt were commonly used and 'acceptable' – will very much not be seen as acceptable today. **You** might even be **much more** aware of modern labels and names for things (and why we do and don't use certain words) than they are.

I'm almost certain you will have heard expressions or words used by older people before that you know today are racial slurs, or that are harmful and disrespectful.

And undoubtedly there will be words we use today, and even in this book, that may become outdated at some point. We may, I hope, with more conversation, find better, more accurate and kinder ways to describe ourselves and our experiences together, but for now it might be helpful to look at the language that has been used historically, and where it's come from, to understand why we don't use it any more. This will also help us think about improving our use of words in the future.

Whole or both – not half

In her letter Tori talks about a very useful and inspiring idea that many mixed people have told me they can relate to. The idea of being 'both' and '100% whole', as opposed to half of one thing and half of another.

Often, mixed-race people tell me that they sometimes find that other people try to tell them 'what' they are rather than asking. In fact, sometimes when people ask questions that might make us feel uncomfortable (like the ones we talked about in chapter 1 – remember the Question Burger?) they then later follow them up by telling you 'what' and who they think you are. This happened to my friend fairly often when she was growing up, and I remember her telling me about a time when she got her first job working in a care home. She was telling her colleague that she is mixed Jamaican and white British, and her colleague said, 'No – you're white'.

One of the mistakes people often make when they do this is calling us 'half' – they will say we are 'half of this' and 'half of that' or half of something and half of something else.

> **The problem with the idea of 'half' of something is that it implies that the other half is somehow missing.**

The thing is – like Tori was saying – people can't really be half of something. We are all complete and whole, 100% us, which is why calling someone 'half' can seem a bit unkind to say.

This is also a microaggression. And it's a microaggression that is quite specific to mixed people.

If someone tells you that you are 'half', whether you think they are unintentionally using this microaggression or not, it is a valid response to tell them firmly that you are actually 'not half of anything'. In Tori's case she might reply, 'Actually I am both Chinese and English, and that's why I call myself Eurasian'.

You can go ahead and gently and clearly tell them who you are. If they continue to use this expression, you can even ask them not to.

EXAMPLE

When you're mixed-race it can sometimes feel as if you're straddling two worlds, balancing on a tightrope trying to keep everyone happy with who you are, and this can make it difficult for you to have a stable and comfortable way to define and describe yourself to others. Other people questioning who and 'what' we are can raise a lot of questions. It can prompt you to ask yourself, 'But where do I fit in?'

In Tori's letter, she talks about why it's been important for her to find a term to describe herself that fits her. A way that feels right for celebrating the beauty of her dual heritage that more accurately represents the 'cool ways in which these two cultures (Chinese and British) collide and mix together'. She talks about how finding the word Eurasian to describe herself and her identity made her feel good about being mixed, and reassured her that her parts of herself are not separate – but that instead she is WHOLE.

Another thing Tori mentions that I REALLY relate to – and I wonder if you will too as you go on this journey – is the idea of finding friends in other mixed-race people and feeling a sense of belonging when we share our experiences. Finding ways we feel happy to talk about ourselves can really help us expand our worlds as we have more and more conversations about our own stories and the interesting stories of others along the way. That's why each of these chapters starts with a letter from someone from the mixed-race community. I'm really hoping you'll feel inspired or better understood when you read them.

While we are on this subject and in this chapter, I'd also love to talk about some new terms and descriptors that might help you put a name to things you might be experiencing or feeling. We will also talk about some of the words that you might like people to move away from using, and get a better understanding of why we shouldn't use them. Hopefully these words will make the exercise in the next chapter – 'The Chat' – easier too!

Mixed-race

When I started working on my podcast *Mixed Up* with my co-host Nicole Ocran, we had quite a long conversation about what language or terms we would use to talk about ourselves and the other mixed people we were going to invite onto the podcast. We landed on the phrase **mixed-race** as most comfortable for us personally.

I grew up with this phrase, so to me it reflects the meaning and experience of people in my generation. There might be a term that you prefer or that you feel more comfortable with, and so it's fine to switch this one out for that if it feels right.

Mixed-race is a term we heard a lot when I was younger. We would see the word 'Mixed' on those little forms we are always asked to fill out in waiting rooms, or for official documents and surveys – you know the ones?

The ones where they make you tick things like:

- [ ] **Mixed White/Black Caribbean,**
or
- [ ] **Mixed White/Black African**
or
- [ ] **Mixed/Other**

When I was growing up, I think people assumed that if you were not white but you had lighter brown skin and non-white features, you must be 'mixed-race' – and so they would call you that.

Today I personally still feel comfortable using this phrase but some people feel less and less comfortable with it, and this is for a number of reasons.

The first reason is that as people have become more and more knowledgeable about 'race' and 'ethnicity' and 'heritage' they have more clearly understood that 'race' as we understand it today is a concept that was invented in the nineteenth century. It's really important to note that:

'race' is not a scientific term.

This means that there is no scientific basis for saying that one person is different from another because of their skin colour. Someone thought up the idea of 'race' to be able to explain differences between people who are white and people who are not, and to then be able to give a lot more importance to these differences than they should.

The second reason is that the idea of 'race' was designed for a sinister reason – in order to create control by white people over non-white people – for what were called **'colonial projects'**.

COLONIAL PROJECTS

Activities carried out by governments focused on justifying the takeover and theft of land owned by native people – those who have historically lived on and looked after these places for generations. These projects are set up to maintain an unequal access to wealth between the colonizer (often, but not always white people who took over other people's land) and the colonized (often non-white) people who were originally living on lands that were stolen.

This was to make sure that, in general, society would hold racist attitudes, which made it much easier for **prejudice** to flourish and grow. This meant that truly awful things like slavery could happen without too much challenge. This same concept – the false idea that white people are better than others – enabled slavery in England and the US to continue for hundreds of years.

QUICK DICTIONARY PULL-OUT

PREJUDICE

When someone makes a negative judgement about a person without getting to know them as an individual. People can have prejudices based on, for example: someone's gender, skin colour, how much money someone has or where they're from. The prejudice might result in unfriendly feelings or behaviours directed at an individual or a group.

Essentially, the idea of 'race' was created to invent a hierarchy or pyramid of power, where white people sat at the top, with Black people sitting at the bottom and everyone else somewhere in between.

The reason some people don't like to use the term mixed-race is because they believe it supports the idea that 'race' is a scientific truth. I understand this, but I think we also need to remember that because people have been using the language of race for a long time, the things that we experience while we are seen by others as East Asian or as Black or as Indian feel very real to us. This gives 'race' very real meaning to us as we move through our everyday worlds, and so 'race' cannot just be ignored or dismissed as a made-up thing. An example of this playing out might be the way that people in Britain who are not white are often asked,

> **'Where are you from?'**

because they are seen as different. They are **racialized**. And the reaction to the way they are **racialized** is very real, expressed by others through this question, which might feel alienating.

It is also worth telling you that mixed-race is one of the most used terms to describe us by people such as teachers and academics, and within schools and research documents, and it was also the chosen term for the first academic journal that studied being 'mixed-race'.

Turn the page to read about some more terms people have and – in some cases – still do use to describe mixed-race people.

BIRACIAL

Biracial describes someone of two races ('bi' comes from the Latin word for 'two'). While this is a commonly used term in the US, some people might find this phrase a little limiting, as often we are even more mixed than that. For example, I know that I am mixed Jamaican, originally Sub-Saharan African and Nigerian, with German-Swiss and Cornish ancestry too.

MIXED HERITAGE

This is a term that a social worker told me they use more commonly in their profession in the UK. They like this term as it avoids using 'race'. This is because they want to make it clear that they realize that the concept of 'race' was originally a made-up thing.

MESTIZO (TISOY)

Mestizo, is now often used in the Philippines to describe someone of mixed or fair skin and usually of Spanish or Chinese mixed ancestry. It is shortened to Tisoy in casual language and is a commonly used term by Filipinos to describe mixed-race people. Whilst it means 'mixed' in Spanish as a direct translation, we should be careful with its use as it can hold more negative and derogatory meaning in mainland Spain and in other Latin countries when being used to describe mixed heritage people.

MULTIRACIAL

Multiracial describes someone who has parents or ancestors of multiple different racial or ethnic backgrounds.

INDIGENOUS

Indigenous peoples are social and cultural groups that share collective ancestral ties to certain lands and natural resources where they live, occupy or that they have been displaced or moved away from against their will by governmental or business forces. Some examples of Indigenous groups across the world include the Maya in Central America, the Sámi in northern Europe, and the Māori of New Zealand.

HĀFU

The term hāfu has been used in Japan since the 1970s to indicate mixed-race Japanese people who have one Japanese parent and one non-Japanese parent. It comes from the English word 'half' and means half Japanese.

Some people who are mixed Japanese dislike this term and prefer 'daburu' which means 'double', or 'mikkusu' which translates to 'mixed'.

According to the 2018 government survey, 98% of the population is considered to be of full Japanese heritage. That's why people who look a little different attract more attention there.

HAPA

Hapa is a Hawaiian word for someone of multiracial ancestry. In Hawaii, the word means any person of mixed ethnic heritage, regardless of the specific mix. It is used for any multiracial person of partial East Asian, Southeast Asian, or Pacific Islander mixture in California.

DAINJONG

Meaning biracial or mixed heritage, this is a neutral way to describe mixed people in South Korea. Honhyeol is also used, it translates to something like 'blended' and can be received as positive, neutral or negative depending on context. For example, after the Korean war (1950–1953) Honhyeol individuals often faced prejudice. But now attitudes are changing a bit in South Korea with the notoriety of more mixed-race celebrities and notable people.

Racial legitimization

Have you ever felt like someone is questioning you when you tell them about your background? When you tell them about the different places your parents are from or when you describe your ancestry? How do you feel when this happens?

Many mixed-race people I've spoken to have told me about occasions when they have experienced this, and how it made them feel uncomfortable.

Here's an example of what I mean. A friend of mine is mixed-race Japanese and white British. She has a house in Japan and goes there often, she speaks Japanese and is very connected to the Japanese culture and community. She also has blonde hair and she has a very pale skin

WAVING CAT

The 'Chinese waving cat' is a well-known kitsch ornament and can be bought in shops around the world. However these cute little statues aren't Chinese at all: they're Japanese.

Named *maneki-neko* in Japanese, meaning 'beckoning cat', the figurine is not actually waving. In Japan, the way to beckon someone over to you is palm forward, fingers pointing down.

tone. She told me about a time when she went to visit a Japanese art exhibition in a Japanese community space in London. A man there was talking to her and when she expressed the fact that she is Japanese mixed white British, he kept saying 'no, that's not true'. She told me that he was almost arguing with her about it, so much so, that eventually she felt she had to **prove** she is Japanese to him, by speaking a little Japanese first, and then when that didn't seem to work by explaining that her mother is Japanese, and then eventually by sharing a lot of the things she knows about Japanese food and places and things.

She said it was exhausting and left her feeling very frustrated.

This is called **'racial legitimization'**. It is where someone doesn't believe you are part of one of your mixed-race groups and you then feel like you have to prove it to them. And although this may feel uncomfortable and put you under pressure if it happens – it's important to remember you don't **actually** have to prove anything about your identity to anyone. Although it can be diffficult when people challenge parts of our identity, all that matters is that you know who you are. If you think you have experienced this before you might like to try the exercise below with your parents or a friend.

EXERCISE NO. 2

Read these questions aloud with your parents or a friend.

Q Have you ever felt like someone is questioning you when you tell them about your background, when you tell them about the different places your parents are from or when you describe your ancestry?

Q Do you ever feel like you need to prove that you belong to one of your mixed-race groups in order to be able to say I am mixed _____ and _____ ?

If so, how did that make you feel?

Q Is there anything you might want to do to handle the situation differently if it happens again?

Misidentification

This is when someone doesn't correctly identify your mix.

This probably happens in people's heads **a lot**. They look at you and decide immediately what they think your mix is. And for the most part, this is kind of harmless right?

The problem is when they don't ask you before they voice what they are thinking – only you have the power to decide your identity – or if they exclude you from a group activity because they don't realize you are part of the group. It can feel quite frustrating or irritating, especially if it happens often. It may mean you don't feel like you are a part of certain groups because of it and this can be upsetting.

> **That feeling is valid – because you are being 'misidentified'.**

Horizontal hostility

Have you ever felt excluded from one of the groups you belong to, like I described above? Have you felt like people from one of the groups of your mix are responding negatively to you when you would expect them to be supportive and able to understand you better than others might?

Japanese mixed people living in Japan have reported this has happened to them, and this could be related to what I mentioned above – that about 98% of the population identify as being of 100% Japanese heritage. Mixed heritage people who look different may be treated as if they don't belong, even if they are Japanese nationals.

We would call this **horizontal hostility**. This is when people in the same group are rude to or unaccepting of one another. Imagine yourself on a sports team – like football or hockey – about to play a game, and all of your team are on one side of a pitch. But instead of feeling the hostility and competitiveness of your team focused towards the other team on the other side of the pitch, you feel it focused towards you. This is why it's called horizontal hostility.

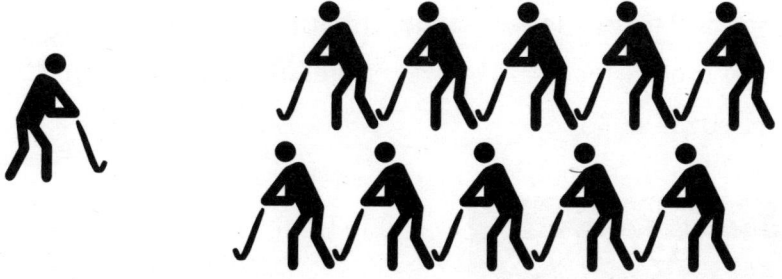

Cultural homelessness

This is when we experience discomfort because we feel as if we are not being received as part of one or more of our cultures. You might feel this when someone who is important to you has expectations of you in regards to how you express your identity that don't match up with how you want to express it.

An example of this might be if your parents expect you to push the part of the culture you share with them forward into the world and display it with pride at all times – for example by by eating certain foods or dressing a certain way – in a way that makes you feel uncomfortable. It could be that what they are asking of you makes you feel isolated from another group of people – like our friends or our other parent. This might feel uncomfortable and maybe even lonely.

EXERCISE NO.3

Imagine Mila, whose mum is Korean and whose dad is Nigerian. She was born in France, lives in Britain and speaks English at school, Korean with her mum at home, and Yoruba (a Nigerian dialect) with her dad.

- When Mila visits Korea, people say she's **'too dark to be Korean'**.

- In Nigeria, some people call her **'Oyinbo'**, which means foreigner or white person.

- And in Britain, classmates ask, **'Where are you really from?'**

Even though she belongs to all these cultures, Mila feels like she doesn't fully belong in any of them. That's what cultural homelessness feels like.

Now think about and note down any experiences that have made you feel this way. Or if you don't think you've experienced this feeling, reverse the exercise and note down the times that have really made you feel like you belong to one or more of your cultural groups.

For example, you might want to take inspiration from Tori who said telling her story to friends and hearing theirs made her feel a sense of belonging, or from Dean who said learning to cook his parents' recipes from Cyprus and Jamaica made him feel close to his heritage.

Outdated discriminatory terms

I still remember really clearly the day I came home from primary school at about seven or eight years old, and telling my mum that I was 'half-caste'. I remember her being furious and asking me who had told me this. Where had I learnt this word? I ended up sharing with her the moment another little girl bounced up to me in the playground announcing that I was 'half-caste'.

I wanted to share this story before we learn about language that is not appropriate to use any more because it's important to know when people might be using a derogatory term to describe you so you can correct them, explain why it's not OK to use this language and tell them how you describe yourself.

HALF-CASTE

This is an offensive term that comes from the term 'caste', which comes from the Latin 'castus', which means 'pure'. You can see that to call someone half-pure is extremely rude and demeaning. 'Caste' also comes from the Portuguese word 'casta', meaning 'lineage' or 'breed'.

The term started being used during the time when Europe was ruling over places like India, the Caribbean, and Africa (becoming common in the mid-1800s) and governments were grouping people based on racial ancestry.

BROWNING

This is a Jamaican Patois word for mixed people that refers to skin colour. It's often used to describe someone with lighter skin. We don't use the term any more because it comes from colourism where people give preference to those with lighter skin.

MULATTO

Mulatto has been used to refer to people of mixed African and European ancestry. In English and European countries the term is seen as a very negative way to describe mixed people because people who study language believe that it comes from the Portuguese word 'mula' (from the Latin 'mūlus'), meaning 'mule', the child of a horse and a donkey. However, some Latin Americans use this term as a source of pride.

Today there are some people who are trying to reclaim the term in popular culture – for example Latto, the American rapper who is using a shortening of the word as her stage name. She was previously going by Miss Mulatto but she confirmed that she changed her name to Latto in response to the negative ideas around the word Mulatto. She said that she wanted to change the feeling around the term and flip it into a positive, but she understands why people still feel it is offensive.

WHITE PASSING

Racial passing occurs when a person who is a member of one racial group is accepted or perceived as a member of another racial group. White passing is where someone whose ancestry is not white is seen by white people as white, and therefore they could – if they wanted to – move through their life as though they are white.

Historically, and especially during times of slavery, being 'white passing' had a different and much more impactful meaning. During these times, which in America were known as Antebellum Slavery (1861–1865), passing as white could mean escaping slavery. Enslaved people who were very light in skin tone might run away from their captors and hide within white society, living their lives as a white person. Through doing this they could remain free. But they would need to leave their families behind and live a lie, denying their true selves and who they really are for the rest of their lives just to be safe.

Some mixed people really dislike this term being used now because it feels like it ignores the truth of who they are — remember Becca the DJ and how someone tried to deny her heritage?

The term also implies that someone would want to try to be white, that it's a positive thing, and that they have achieved something by being seen as white and that feels very uncomfortable for a lot of people.

MUWALLADEEN

The term Muwalladeen refers to Yemenis who are of mixed origins (with a Yemeni father or grandfather and a non-Yemeni mother or grandmother). The term is often used in a derogatory way, and Muwalladeen have been the target of discriminatory practices for decades. They were, and still are, often denied rights by their country, and forced to work in bad conditions at work. They often face prejudice from people socially and sometimes they don't have access to proper schooling. Muwalladeen often pretend that they aren't mixed-race in order to avoid exclusion. This is particularly true for those whose families have links with Africa; Muwalladeen of mixed Yemeni-African descent are more racialized than Muwalladeen of other backgrounds, such as those whose families have historical links with Asia or Europe.

Useful ideas

BOTH NOT HALF

A friend of mine, Jassa Ahluwalia, who is of Punjabi and English heritage, came up with a really empowering phrase and concept that I think is very useful when thinking about the language you might want to use to talk about your own identity – 'both not half'.

It means that a person who has mixed heritage is fully

both (or all) of their backgrounds – not half of one and half of another. It disagrees with the idea that mixed people are somehow incomplete, or not 'fully' anything.

BOTH/AND

This is another version of the 'both not half' idea and gives us a way to talk about ourselves that recognizes that we can be two things at once. For example, I am Black and I am mixed. I am proud to be both of these things.

MONORACIAL

This is used to describe someone of one race. 'Mono' translates to 'one'. This isn't my favourite term as it feels kind of scientific and as we've discussed, **race is not science**.

LIGHT SKINNED

A term that is commonly confused with being similar to or the same as being mixed-race. Some people use it as a shorthand for mixed-race, but this is not accurate. 'Light skinned' means someone who has a lighter skin tone, but being a lighter skin tone doesn't always mean you are mixed-race or identify as mixed-race.

3
The Chat

Fola Evans-Akingbola

is an actress of British-Nigerian heritage and a BAFTA-nominated filmmaker of *Untold Stories: Hair on Set*, championing inclusivity.

Dear Reader,

A taxi pulls up outside my house and I step in. The Nigerian driver spies my obviously Yoruba first name, Fola, and then scans to my surname – Evans-Akingbola – with Welsh 'Evans' paired to Yoruba 'Akingbola'. He glances back at me in the rear-view mirror. *Here it comes . . .*

'Which of your parents is Black? Do you speak Yoruba?'

'No,' I reply.

'Ah, that's because your mum is white. What food was cooked in your house growing up? You don't look Nigerian.'

To which I always respond, 'What does Nigerian look like?'

Our names are one of the first ways people encounter us, whether on the attendance register at school, meeting new people at work or getting into an Uber. It is part of the way we make sense of each other's histories. My parents' decision to give my sister and me Yoruba first names and a double-barrelled surname, rooted me in the different aspects of my heritage and speaks volumes about a household which didn't shy away from speaking about identity.

Already woven into the very fabric of who I am by my name, I received the message that I am a wonderful combination of my parents and all our ancestors, and I do not have to choose between them. To understand myself fully, no aspect of my heritage needs be denied or reduced. I learnt that there is beauty in difference and in valuing all those differences equally.

So in reality, there was no one singular 'chat' in our home. It was an environment that encouraged an ongoing exploration of identity and belonging. It was outside the home that I had the many 'chats' about my mixed-race heritage, brought up by taxi drivers, teachers, colleagues, lovers, friends and complete strangers.

From a young age I chose to embrace questions like 'What is your heritage?' and 'Where are you from?' No matter what the person asking looks like, I always ask them in return, 'What about you, what is your heritage?' Sometimes this becomes an opportunity to have a chat with someone who is not used to having questions about identity, race and belonging turned around for them to reflect on.

Fola

As we've discussed in the last chapter, sometimes when we are growing and learning about ourselves there will be things we find difficult to talk about. Particularly when it comes to our sense of who we are. That's totally normal.

It's normal to feel as if you're struggling to pluck up the courage to talk about this stuff with your friends or your parents, especially if you're the first one to bring it up.

But it's really important to try to talk about your identity and who you are. It can help you to build connections with different parts of your cultures and build self-confidence. As Fola shows us with her story about the taxi driver, and many other people who have wanted to chat with her about her identity, there may be times when people approach this conversation in what feels like an unkind or thoughtless way. For example, it was definitely impolite and probably hurtful to suggest that it is Fola's mum's fault that she doesn't speak Yoruba. If we can find a way to embrace the conversation, it can become a wonderful opportunity to explore what we think and feel about our own identity. It can also provide a way for us to connect with others who might share parts of our heritage and cultural histories. It can even provide an opportunity to practise gently disagreeing, standing up for ourselves and speaking up about what we understand about our own identity.

I'll let you in on something – I would say that most adults probably find it challenging to talk about their feelings when it comes to discussing subjects like race, cultural differences, ethnicity and who we are in the relation to all this, too. Talking about our identities and how we feel about them can be really hard! If we're being real about it, adults are probably far less used to saying exactly what they think than you are! It might help to remember when you're reading this chapter and thinking about the exercises in it.

> **This chapter is all about how you can help your parents talk to you about being mixed.**

It may be the case that your parents themselves identify as being of mixed heritage, or they might instead think of themselves as 'mono racial' (of only one race) for example, only Black, white, East Asian, South East or South Asian . . . while you think of yourself as mixed because you have two parents who both have different racial and/or ethnic backgrounds.

With that in mind, your parents or family members may not quite be sure how to open up a conversation with you about how you're feeling about your identity. They might be scared of 'getting it wrong', of upsetting you or even of having to talk about something that they experienced with race or their heritage that didn't feel good for them. There are lots of reasons why they might find this conversation difficult. Perhaps they are simply struggling to find the right words, but that's OK because you've **DEFINITELY** got this after all the things you read in the last chapter. Just remember that, most of the time, the people in your life will be really happy that you've started the conversation, so it's worth being brave and trying.

Right! Now we are feeling ready to get started – let's work on some ways to take the bull by the horns and open up the conversation ourselves!

Remember that if you're finding it difficult to find the words to start this conversation, you can ask your friends or family to read this chapter, so they can get the inside track.

Grab a pen and some paper, copy the sentences on the next page, and fill in the gaps. Take your time to really consider what you want to say.

From speaking to people on my podcast and through reading other books by psychologists and other experts, I've managed to learn some more language to help me have these conversations. I'm going to talk about some of the key phrases and their meanings with you so that you can use them too. The first word I want to talk about is **misidentification**. We've actually already come across this word in the previous chapter 'Language Matters', but I want to give this idea a bit more context so I've asked my friend Jassa (who I also mentioned in the previous chapter) to talk about his experiences. This will help us really understand what being misidentified might look and feel like in an everyday scenario.

EXERCISE NO.4

CONVERSATION STARTER QUESTIONS:

How do you see yourself? I see myself as _____

What do you notice about your race? _____

It feels _____ to be part of _____ and _____ groups at the same time.

Because I look a certain way, sometimes people think _____ but that's not how I see myself.

Sometimes I feel like I have to prove to other people that I am part of one of these groups and it makes me feel _____.

I feel really proud of what you/Dad/Nan/Lola/Abuela/Babushka taught me about _____ in our shared heritage but I don't know much about _____.

Jassa Ahluwalia

is a British actor and author of Both Not Half. He was born in Coventry to a white English mum and brown Punjabi dad.

Dear Reader,

You are whole and multiple, but have been born into a world built on separation and fractions. You are both, not half. You are all, not part. Our misguided society forces us to ask ourselves: who am I? But do not despair. We must count ourselves lucky. This is the only question worth asking. We are on an epic adventure. We are on the path to discovering **who we are**. And by our very existence, we are here to change the world.

I am Punjabi and English. I have a brown dad and a white mum. I speak Punjabi and grew up immersed in Punjabi culture. But I look very white. I have spent much of my life being told that I do not 'look Indian', and I've been frequently made to feel like I need to explain myself, as if someone else's assumption is more important than reality.

Once, when I was very ill, hospital staff made assumptions based on my name and failed to identify me. I was in a lot of pain, I could've died, but that feeling of invisibility is the most painful memory of all. When I finally recovered, I made it my mission to assert my identity in the world.

Your mixed identity is a blinding light. It has the power to banish ignorance. There are no separate races, only one **human race**. Your very existence is a testament to the unity of humankind. Sadly, so long as there is ignorance in the world, you may be misidentified. But you do not have to take responsibility for other people's discomfort and confusion. You do not need to apologize. You do not need to explain. **They** need to **listen**. **They** need to **learn**. You are the only authority on your identity that matters. Tell the world who you are.

In solidarity,

Jassa Ahluwalia ★

As Jassa points out, if someone misidentifies you, they are making a false assumption about you, but that assumption can never be more important than the reality of what you know about your heritage and who you are. Jassa says in his letter that when he was misidentified in hospital he felt 'invisible'. What a horrible way to make someone feel! I don't think any of us would want to feel that way, or would want to make someone else feel like they are unimportant and quite literally not seen or acknowledged by us.

As Jassa tells us, there are multiple empowering things we can refer to or hold on to if something like this happens.

> **The first thing to remember is that we are 'both, not half' — we do not have to agree to other people's ideas of us being only part of something.**

Jassa wholly embraces his Indian heritage – speaking the language, dancing traditional Punjabi dance and surrounding himself in the culture, so no one has the right to tell him that he doesn't have a place in his Indian community.

As Jassa also points out in his letter above, we are all on an epic adventure of discovery and it's OK to not have all the answers yet. It's OK to explore different ways of describing yourself as you discover new words and phrases. I think ultimately his point is that as you are learning, they can learn, too.

EXAMPLE

Another example of misidentification happened to my friend Jack Fowler – a presenter and DJ I've interviewed on my podcast – who told me about something that happened to him when he was younger. His football coach said some prejudiced things about Black boys in front of him. The coach 'misidentified' him as white, even though Jack's Dad is Black and from St Helena; in actuality, Jack is mixed-race. Jack was only eight years old at the time but he still remembers this moment vividly, because being misidentified can be really painful.

Misidentification can feel isolating and frustrating. It's even harmful to not be recognized as part of one or more of the groups you belong to. Sometimes it can even make people feel comfortable being racist or unkind towards one of the groups you belong to, right in front of you. If you feel safe to do so, it's important to tell them that this is **not OK**.

These experiences can be helpful to share with your

parents, as they may not have first-hand experience of this kind of thing.

Using the language we learnt in the previous chapter, try applying the following prompts to help your parents, friends or family talk to you about your identity.

EXERCISE NO.5

CONTINUING THE CONVERSATION

Thinking about the language we learnt in the last chapter, are there any experiences you've had that you think your parents might not understand?

Can you use any of the language below to talk to them about these experiences?

- **Racial legitimization**
- **Misidentification**
- **Horizontal hostility**
- **Cultural homelessness**

4

The History of the Mixed Experience

India Amarteifio

is a British actress. She grew up in the UK with her white mum and her dad who is Black — born in London, with Ghanian ancentry.

Dear Reader,

MIXED-RACE PEOPLE HAVE BEEN IN EXISTENCE FOREVER!

Just because history and art have erased us, it doesn't mean we haven't been around. I found out more about this when I played the role of Queen Charlotte, who was queen of Britain and Ireland (1761–1818). There is much speculation as to her heritage, many historians believe she was of African descent, but her skin would have been painted lighter in portraits to keep from causing scandal at the time! We can see evidence of this maybe being true from early portraits of her and the fact that her features are unlike others from the continent. How cool, right?

It made me feel so inspired to be able to act out that portion of history in a way that makes others that look like me feel as regal as I felt portraying her. I grew up in a community with not many other mixed-race people around, so I always felt a little out of place. If I knew that a past figure of such great stature could have looked like me when I was a kid, it would have made me feel a lot more at home in my home. Our mixed backgrounds are what make us unique, and that is visible even 300 years ago.

Keep being you!

India :) ☆

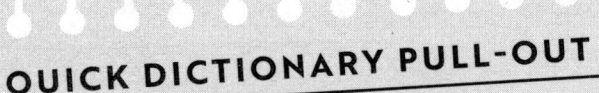

QUICK DICTIONARY PULL-OUT

DEMOGRAPHIC

A section or specific group of the population.

One of the most exciting things I discovered through all my conversations and research around mixed-race people is that we are the fastest growing **demographic** (or group of people) in the UK and US. I think that's pretty cool! It means there are so many other mixed-race people out there to connect with and find out about. On top of that, I am learning that collectively as a group, across all backgrounds, we have a rich history that a lot of people are not aware of!

In the UK, based on the 2021 national census we make up 2.9 per cent of the population (that's roughly 1.7 million people!).

You might be surprised to know that mixed-race people have existed in Britain in large numbers from as early as the 1500s. You might have learnt about this era in your history classes as the **'Renaissance Era'** – the century described by many historians as the rise of Western civilization and characterized by an abundance of creativity, art, science and wealth.

This era was really quite early on in the history books – I'm talking around the time of the Tudors, Henry VIII, Queen Elizabeth I and the Stuarts. So you see – as India jokes in her letter – **we existed in our numbers, in Britain, much earlier than people might expect ('forever!'), and there are stories of specific people to prove it!**

In 1578, we have record of a Captain George Best commenting that he had **'seen an Ethiopian as black as coal brought to England, who taking a fair English woman to wife, begat a son in all respects as black as the father'.**

In 1694, a writer named Charles Gildon noted that **'experience tells us there's nothing more common than matches of this kind, where the whites and the blacks cohabit'.**

14th – 16th Century

14th Century: Renaissance, marking a move from the Middle Ages to modernity with innovation and exploration, begins in Italy.

1485: Tudor dynasty, characterized by religious and political changes and a flourishing of the arts and travel, begins in England.

c. 1527: The Sack of Rome marks the end of the Italian High Renaissance.

In the eighteenth century (the Age of Enlightenment), author Philip Thicknesse wrote of his prejudice and discomfort with the idea that in **'every country town, nay, in almost every village are to be seen a little race of mulattoes, mischievous as monkeys, and infinitely more dangerous.'**

These examples show that mixed-race families existed hundreds of years ago — even though many people at the time didn't understand or respect them.

This is a good example of what we were discussing in the last chapter about how terms and words used to describe different groups are constantly changing, and what is acceptable and not changes drastically over time. You can see from these quotes just how much language has evolved since Charles, George and Phillip noted the mixed people they were coming across.

There are some very specific moments in time that it's important to pull out and reference, to give a little bit more of an understanding around the historical experiences of mixed-race people and their families – not only in Britain, but around the world.

As we look at how mixed-race families and people were living, and discover their stories throughout history, it might be interesting to watch closely as to the way that they were thought about by other people. Can you chart how society changes and shifts over time, and why?

Ivory Bangle Lady around mid-4th century

'Ivory Bangle Lady' is the name of a skeleton of a woman who lived in the Roman times and was thought to be mixed-race – specifically of Black and white ancestry. Her skeleton was found in York in 1901, buried in a coffin alongside expensive jewellery and other items. From this, historians deduced that she was

4th–5th centuries

395: the Roman Empire is divided into the West and East.

c. 410: Roman rule officially ends in Britain.

476: the fall of the Western Roman Empire.

not only wealthy, but from a North African and upper-class background. Despite the fact that the Roman Empire was over 1,500 years ago, it was a time when social status was not determined by the colour of your skin. So, it would not have been strange for a Black or mixed-race person to have been wealthy.

Dido Elizabeth Belle (1761–1804)

Dido Elizabeth Belle's mother was an enslaved African woman named Maria Belle and her father was called Sir John Lindsay, a British naval officer stationed in the Caribbean. Belle was born in the Caribbean in 1761, born into slavery to parents who were not married. Belle's father brought her and her Black mother to England when she was four years old. It was in Georgian Britain where Belle eventually lived as a free gentlewoman – educated and raised by her uncle Lord Mansfield, who was a judge. At this time, it was not unusual for male colonists who had children with enslaved women to bring them to England, and often the Black enslaved women didn't have a choice.

There is one known portrait of Belle which lives in Scone Palace, Scotland. Art historians believe it can tell us a little bit about how she lived her life – she was well educated and most likely lived as a companion for her white cousin, Lady Elizabeth Murray. As a companion, she was expected to provide company and conversation to her cousin, but she was not seen as equal to her. Unusual for the time, she is painted at the same height level as her white cousin, which could tell us that she was respected within the family, despite the fact she was a mixed-race Black woman. (Back then it was common for people who were thought to be more important, of noble or royal blood, to be depicted higher up in portraits.)

Though her cousin is in the forefront of the portrait – which acknowledges the difference in status applied to white women versus women of colour at the time – her cousin also appears to reach for her affectionately, which gives us a sense that she commanded some respect and was not treated as completely inferior within the household she grew up in. At the time this would have been quite unusual, because commonly people thought of white Europeans as superior to any person of colour, especially because Britain was so heavily involved in the slave trade and the enslavement of Black men and women. It was not generally accepted that white and Black men and women would marry each other or have children together, and certainly not among the upper class.

Mary Seacole (1805–81)

Mary Seacole is still today one of the most famous Black, mixed Jamaicans. She identified as 'Creole', which means mixed European and Black Caribbean descent, and she learnt traditional herbal medicine from her mother in Jamaica. She broke social rules and norms and defied prejudices to travel the world, run businesses and help those in need – even in very dangerous places and circumstances. She is best known for her work as a nurse in the Crimean War (1853–56).

Cardiff – Tiger Bay

The area in Wales formerly known as Tiger Bay (now Cardiff Bay) is the site of one of the UK's oldest multicultural communities. Between 1800 and 1901, it was fast growing with migrant communities from over fifty nationalities, including Norwegian, Greek, Somali, Yemeni, Spanish, Italian, Caribbean and Irish.

Because it was a port city that developed as a hub to export coal, working seamen arrived from all over the world to live and work there – in this unique place that had become a multicultural community. From as far back as the 1830s, residents of many races and backgrounds socialized together, fell in love, got married and had children, creating this distinct community where many mixed-race children were born and grew up among similar families.

There were, however, a lot of people who disapproved of Tiger Bay and other places in the UK that were seeing a rise in mixed-race children from interracial marriages. In the early twentieth century, a local Chief Constable

Rumney

Cardiff Bay

Splott Beach

Ferry Court

Penarth

Dinas Powys

Lavernock

Wilson became famous for his negative ideas about the Tiger Bay community. He said, 'Half-caste children had a vicious hereditary taint of their parents, meaning that they would be certain to inherit issues and problems simply because they were mixed race. The time may come when public opinion will awaken to the fact that our race has become leavened with the coloured strain. Someone must have the courage to strike a warning note.'

Chief Constable Wilson called for Wales to look at South Africa's Apartheid movement.

Constable Wilson was so concerned by Tiger Bay's reputation for immorality and mixed-race marriages that he wrote to his local police committee saying that these relationships were wrong. He suggested that the presence of non-white seamen in the town was a real problem and he wanted the police to help stop these marriages and relationships.

APARTHEID AND SOUTH AFRICA'S HISTORY WITH RACE

Apartheid was a system developed in South Africa and used from 1948 until 1994 where people were treated unfairly based on their skin colour:

- People with white skin (called 'Europeans') had the most power and the best jobs, houses and schools.
- People with black, brown or pigmented skin tones were treated as lower class and had less advantages. They had to live in separate areas called townships and go to different schools. They couldn't always live where they wanted, and they had to carry passes just to walk around the country.
- Apartheid laws separated these groups and made it very hard for people of colour to get the same chances as white people.
- Those laws also stopped people from the different groups getting married or having children together, which meant that it was technically illegal to have a mixed-race child during Apartheid in South Africa.

A little later, during the Second World War, Tiger Bay yet again had an interesting part to play in the history of multiculturalism and mixed-race people in the UK.

QUICK DICTIONARY PULL-OUT
MULTICULTURALISM

When people from different backgrounds, with different skin colours, languages and traditions can all live together and share their unique ways of doing things, like celebrating holidays or eating different foods.

During the Second World War many African American soldiers in the US Army were stationed across the UK, although the Army gave strict **segregation** rules to prevent these Black soldiers from having relationships with white women (due to racism, interracial couples were seen as socially unacceptable at the time). Many of the women of Tiger Bay came from mixed backgrounds themselves having, for example, Yemeni and Irish parents, and so to them multiculturalism was normal and commonplace in their communities.

The army tried to keep the American soldiers and the women of Tiger Bay apart by forbidding the soldiers to go into Tiger Bay. But as the story goes, local people would ferry the soldiers back and forth from Tiger Bay to visit their girlfriends. People fell in love and had children together. Sadly, when the war ended the couples were often separated, and many mothers were encouraged to give up their children for adoption. Some were brought up in Tiger Bay, but often they were looked down upon by wider society for being mixed-race.

SEGREGATION: the separation of different groups of people, maybe through different races, religions, or genders.

Do you know the singer Shirley Bassey? She's a fantastic Welsh singer and entertainer – who even sang some James Bond theme tunes! (Ask your mum or dad – they will know what I'm on about.) Bassey was born in Tiger Bay in 1937, her father was Nigerian and her mother was British from North Yorkshire. In 1958, she became the first Welsh singer to have a No. 1 hit in the UK chart, and went on to be internationally famous.

Liverpool

It wasn't just Tiger Bay where mixed families and multicultural communities were formed. Mixed-race communities were springing up in sea ports around Britain because seamen of all races and backgrounds, as well as British citizens themselves, had come to the ports to live and work.

Liverpool

Because the British Empire was multicultural, spanning across countries in Asia, Africa and many more continents, lots of these men were not white. History has taught us that the tragedy of war is almost always sad and needless. It is true, however, that one of the outcomes of war is that they have played a significant role in bringing people of different heritages from where they were born to new homes elsewhere, either to fight for one of the countries at war, or to fill gaps in the community left by workers who went off to fight. While wars have certainly created terrible divisions between different people and cultures, they have also brought about unexpected encounters and relationships.

Liverpool was one of these port cities, and has its own story of unions between Chinese seamen and British women. During the Second World War, around 20,000 Chinese men came to Britain to work in the Navy and in the Liverpudlian shipping industry. Britain desperately needed more hands on deck (pun intended) and these seamen formed an important part of the war effort. Hundreds of Chinese men ended up meeting and marrying British women in Liverpool and starting families with them.

But when the war was over, the government started a secret project to find the men and send them back to China. Using shipping company records, informants and by visiting hotels and lodgings where they suspected these men were staying, the men were kidnapped.
The men – and their wives – had no idea what was happening. It was only decades later, with the opening of government files, that some of the mixed-race children of these men really found out what had happened to their fathers and why they had disappeared.

Sadly, with the men gone – breadwinners of their families at the time – the women were often unable to feed their families, and some were rejected by their own

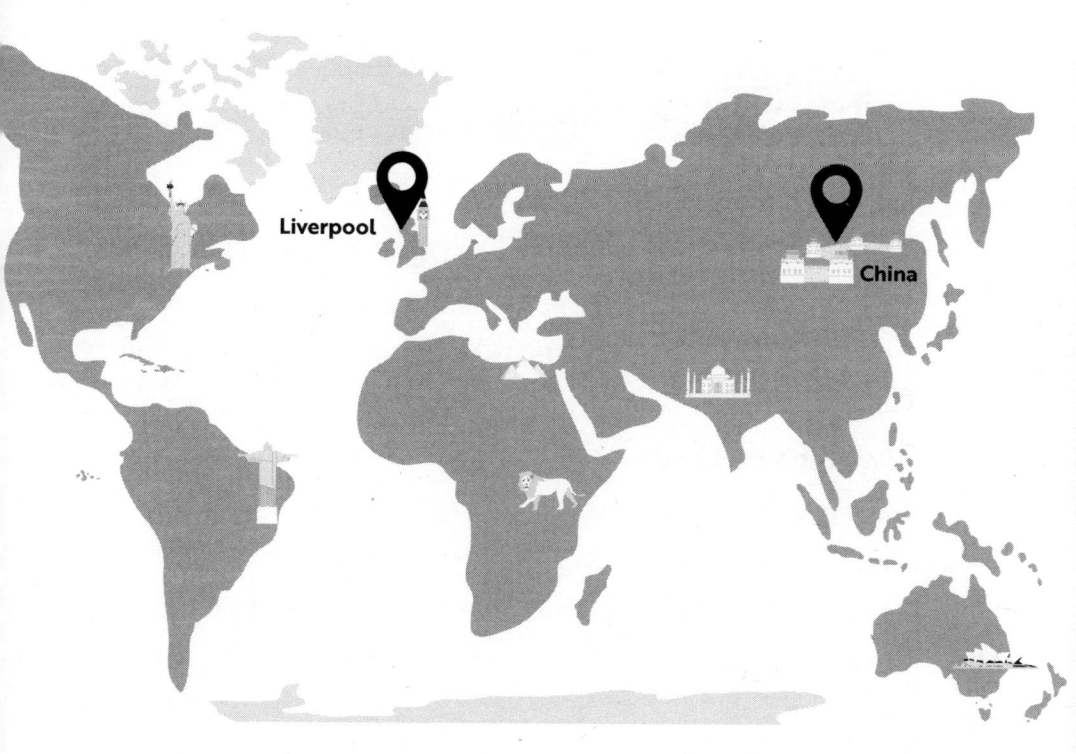

families for having married Chinese men.

In 2022, after decades of silence, the British government and the Labour Party – which was in power at the time – apologized for the forced removal of the Chinese seamen from Britain, recognizing that it had done lasting harm to families, leaving 'scars that have run deep through several generations' the Labour Party said, speaking about the scandal in 2022.

Second World War GI babies

During the Second World War (1939–45), roughly 1 million US army men (GIs) were stationed in England between 1942–45, and more than 100,000 of these men were African American servicemen. Relationships formed between these servicemen and local white women, and subsequently many mixed-race children were born. Interracial marriage was illegal in the US at the time, and so US policy was to refuse these men the right to marry their partners.

As a result, many of these children were born outside of marriage and their mothers were often pressured to give them up for adoption and into care based on the social stigma of having a 'brown baby' – let alone outside of marriage. At the same time, there was a panic spreading across Britain about what the rise in mixed-race children and marriages between people of different races meant for society. This panic was spread by the government and groups who did not want to see more people of colour come to live in the country.

The British government discussed sending the children, who were now in care, to the US to be raised by their fathers, but in the end this plan did not go ahead. In part due to racist attitudes in the UK and US, but also because the children were seen as British citizens, so sending them away  was not popular or easy. Instead, the children were sent to hostels and local organizations, as children's charities such as Barnardo's refused to take children that were not white.

Barnardo's was one of the largest and most influential child welfare organizations in the UK at the time. Their refusal to take mixed-race children effectively blocked one of the main options for their safe care. Once that option was gone, local councils had few places left to send the children. So rather than explore the more difficult and expensive option of sending them to be with family overseas, they took the cheaper route: keeping the children in the UK in care homes and hostels.

Mother and baby institutions in Congo and Ireland

Meanwhile in the Democratic Republic of Congo – formerly a colony of Belgium – interracial relationships were illegal from 1908 to 1960, and babies born out of these unions were seen as the property of Belgium. These babies were labelled the Métis – a term that labelled them as children of European fathers and Congolese mothers – and in a government project where they were kidnapped from their mothers and given to the church to raise or sent for adoption. Their mothers were often told that if they tried to fight back to keep their babies, the other villagers in their communities would be killed.

Democratic Republic of the Congo, Africa

In Ireland, a similar thing was happening. Much like with the white mothers in Britain, pregnant but unmarried women in Ireland – which was, and still is, quite a religious country – were being sent to mother and baby institutions. In the 1940s, there was a high migration of male African students to Ireland, in part, because it was an affordable and renowned place to study. Again, mixed-race unions were formed and babies were conceived.

Unmarried mothers who were pregnant with mixed-race babies were often persuaded – even more heavily than unmarried mothers of white babies – by their parents and families to give up their children. Due to the racist views widely held by society, the government and the church at the time, it was seen as an even greater sin to have a baby of colour than having a baby without being married.

Ireland, UK

Paul McGrath – a renowned Irish footballer – is a good example of this. He was born in Greenford, Middlesex, UK, in December 1959. His mother, Betty McGrath, was from Dublin in Ireland and his father was a Nigerian medical student studying in Dublin. After a brief relationship, Betty became pregnant and, as frequently happened in Ireland during this period, due to the stigma she went to the UK to have her baby.

Betty McGrath came under immense pressure from the nuns at the mother and baby institution in Acton, West London, to put her child up for adoption. Despite refusing, the Catholic Crusade organization in Dublin was contacted to arrange fostering. On her return to Dublin, Betty's son, Paul, was taken away as soon as she arrived. But Betty's commitment to maintaining a relationship with Paul was strong, and she managed to visit regularly and develop a close relationship with her son. Sadly, this kind of pressure was still being put on mothers as late as 1998.

Barbara Beese

Barbara Beese is a British activist known for being part of the Mangrove Nine – a group of Black activists who were arrested, in 1970, after protesting the harassment of the Caribbean restaurant 'The Mangrove' in Notting Hill, London. The nine activists famously went to trial to defend themselves from prosecution. At the end of the trial the judge acknowledged there was evidence of racism. All the defendants were acquitted of the main charges of incitement to riot.

Beese was born in 1946 to a Black father and a teenage white mother. She grew up in the care system, where she was told she was 'too Negroid for adoption'. After running away repeatedly, she was eventually sent to an institution for juvenile delinquents.

NEGROID:
Negroid is an offensive racial slur.

Despite these challenges, she went on to attend teacher training college and eventually met Darcus Howe, who introduced her to the idea of 'Black Power' which she described as a 'homecoming' or the feeling of belonging at last. The visuals of her protesting have become a symbol for British Black protests and she is a well-known figure representing anti-racist activism.

QUICK DICTIONARY PULL-OUT

BLACK POWER

The Black Power group was made up of Black people working together in the 1960s to stand up for their rights. It encouraged **Black people to be proud of who they are,** to **stand up for their rights,** and to **have control over their own communities.**

People in the movement wanted to stop racism and unfair treatment, and they believed that Black people should have the **power to make decisions** about their own lives – in schools, jobs and government. It was also about **celebrating Black culture,** history and beauty.

Australia and the stolen generation

In Australia, from the late 1800s to the late 1900s, the government decided to remove mixed Aboriginal children from their homes and place them in what were called **'residential schools'** – places where they were forced to live away from their families. The Australian government created this repulsive scheme to try to remove the children from Aboriginal culture

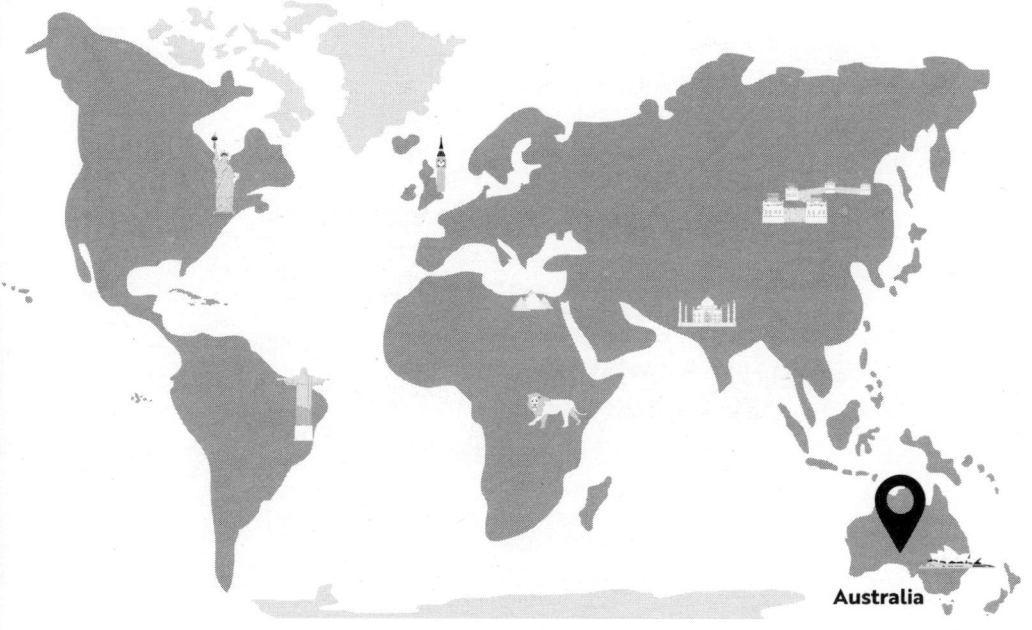

and stop them from learning about their culture. These children were labelled **'The Stolen Generations'**, so you can get a sense of the negative effect it had on society and Aboriginal communities at that time. Ultimately, the government wanted the children to become white children and to distance them from their Aboriginal families and traditions, believing that one day the Aboriginal community would die out.

This was all part of a global political project to deter relationships with people of different races and to keep **white supremacy** in place across the world.

QUICK DICTIONARY PULL-OUT

WHITE SUPREMACY

The belief that white people constitute a superior race and should therefore dominate society. This results in the exclusion of other racial and ethnic groups.

EXERCISE NO.6

You might like to do your own research on other stories about mixed communities and people throughout history.

As you go through the rest of the book, can you find threads and moments of things that interest you? Write them down and make a note to ask a family member to help you find more information about these people or moments from the past.

It's important to remember that this is just a small snippet of the history of mixed-race people. We've highlighted that we existed in lots of different places, but also that we have a lot in common in the ways we have sometimes been received or treated, in recent history particularly.

5
Making Positive Connections

Ashleigh Plumptre

is a professional footballer and was born in Leicester, England. In 2022 Plumptre made a decision to play football for Nigeria, her paternal heritage, over continuing to play for England. It was a heartfelt choice rooted in family and identity.

A letter to little Ash . . .

You're going to go through your childhood years playing every sport you could possibly think of. Your mum will tell everyone she knows that 'she either has a ball at her feet or in her hands at all times'. Any form of 'play' will be your favourite part of the day, and you know what? You were very good at it. It will take you a long old time to realize that you are good at it, but you'll realize that this is part of the journey you're on in uncovering who you really are.

You will start to notice that while football was the game you played for fun, the reason why you play evolves as you grow. From four years old until you stop playing, the confidence you believed you always lacked will show up in every grazed knee, rugged ponytail and hard tackle you make. At fourteen years old, it will start to develop into an unshakable courage to go against the grain. You'll be drawn to leave all your family to study and play football in the US. You are questioned, even threatened, but you go anyway.

You graduate and choose to play professionally for your local team, in spite of having higher calibre teams interested in you. You will be questioned, even threatened, but you go anyway. In 2020, while the world slows down you slow down with it. You start to realize that there is nothing more important in this life than connection to self and connection to others. During this time, you will spend invaluable time with your younger sister, walking, talking and questioning. Through every personal experience shared, tear cried and hope found, a light will turn on. Another piece of your identity will be revealed, and, like every other courageous decision you make, you will forgo your England football ties in the hope of starting a new venture with the Nigerian national team. This will not be without judgement from others, but the more you connect with your interest in learning more about your heritage, the more you are able to deflect any opinion that opposes you on your quest to move closer to your true identity.

You'll realize that this decision will be made, not just for the football reasons, but mainly to delve into your own mixed heritage. This is a part that you won't really question as you go through your youth years, but will start to feel the strong connection to as you become bonded to the harsh lived experiences your loved one has endured so young. Then it will hit you . . . while any expression of who you are is for YOU, it will be tightly experienced and also deeply felt by those you love. It will be a shared journey that binds you even more closely to those you love once you start to peel back the layers of what your heritage teaches you, what it represents and how you choose to live out this connection to your roots.

You'll start to realize that your path was meant to be one only YOU knew and that was just fine.

Through making this decision, you will get on your first ever flight to Nigeria. You will enter the unknown but will feel comforted in knowing that the Nigerian soil welcomes you. That inner knowing will turn to a more tangible feeling. While looking differently than most Nigerians, you are welcomed by Nigerian locals, fans and the team itself. There will be a curiosity from many, but a warmth and gratitude felt both ways as you continue to make yourself available to those who want to know more about you. In the same way they get to learn about you, you are thrust into a completely new environment in the heart of Abuja and have no choice but to learn how to adapt. Unknown to you, you will have to hand-wash your clothes in the hotel sink, share your bed with a teammate and entertain a humbling experience of weeing into a hole on the floor at the field. While it could shock you at first, you remember why you started this journey in the first place. You weren't here for five-star treatment. You were on a quest to go deeper into the parts of you that you have always carried, but also of your relatives and ancestors who came from the soil you also got to step foot on. You realize you have become the combined representation of deep-rooted cultures that are never lost for as long as you continue to respect them.

You realize you do not have to justify your 'Nigerian-ness' to your teammates or anyone for that matter. The best example you have of this is when one of the senior players on the team comes to you after your first international game, puts one hand on your shoulder and says, 'Obim (meaning my love), do you know how I know you are Nigerian? Because you are strong and fight like a Nigerian alongside us on the field.'

This moment will always act as your reminder of how you feel your heritage lives within you and plays out in the way others recognize you. Not from the way you look or the food you prefer, but the traits that you have always felt but never attached to your heritage until you discovered what it means, for you, to be a Nigerian and British girl who likes to play football.

You realize that while your experiences in Nigeria largely contrast those in the UK, they remind you of every aspect of yourself that you couldn't quite associate with living in the UK and being British. Almost like someone pulls back the curtain on part of you that you can connect to and it makes you finally feel found; a deeper connection to self and your own association to the external world.

Ashleigh

I want to talk to you about making connections. And when I say connections, I don't only mean making them with other people, but also with yourself. (That last bit might sound a bit weird, but stick with me.)

I'm talking about the connections we can make to parts of our heritage and the symbols of it – like food, language, clothing, our names, the places our family members are from – and all the things that make you, YOU. We need to make positive connections with ourselves, because that will help us to have great conversations and moments of connection with others across the journeys of our lives.

This is exactly what Ashleigh is getting at when she describes her journey to Nigeria to connect with her Nigerian heritage. She took a really bold decision to leave her home in England to go on an adventure to discover more about her ancestry and the place her dad's family are from. In taking the leap to do this, she made a lot of positive connections – with her fellow Nigerian teammates, with Nigerian culture and language. We can tell from her letter that she even learnt some Igbo!

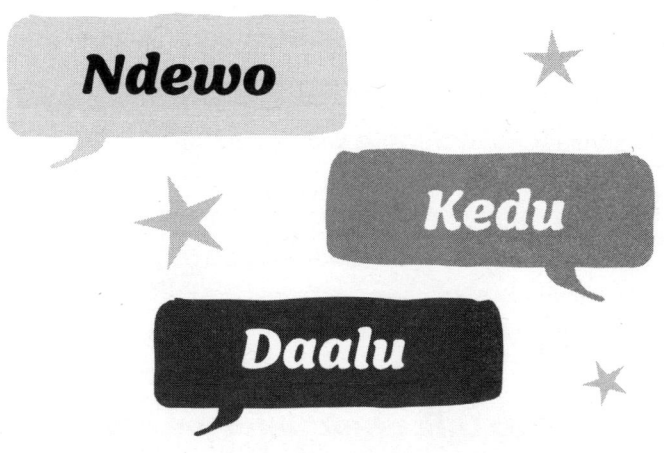

Why is building positive connections with ourselves and others so important?

Building positive connections can help you, over time, with a lot of the things that at first glance might feel very big and overwhelming. In Ashleigh's letter, we can really hear this experience of growing in confidence! But take, for instance, building your confidence or solving problems. Building positive connections with yourself can help you learn about yourself, which in turn makes you feel good about yourself and more confident. Feeling good about yourself and having the confidence to know who you are – what you like and don't like, how you'd like to be treated and how you want to treat others – will help you make strong friendships, which means you'll have people who understand you around when you need to solve a problem.

> **When we are scared to talk about who we are or to ask questions about our identity, it can make it difficult for us to get to know others on a deeper level, and for them to be able to support us when we need it.**

For me, talking openly with other mixed people, as well as my family and friends, about my feelings on being mixed, my experiences and identity have helped me feel safer and more secure in myself. It's helped me to speak up and say when I feel proud of who I am, or when I feel uncomfortable about things someone else may have said. It's like a circle of goodness and positivity. It really helps to talk to people who have been through similar experiences and had similar feelings about their place in the world.

This chapter is also about interesting, fun things you can do to make those positive **connections** to your own heritage and also other people connected to your heritage. Talking to people connected to your heritage (and by this I don't just mean your grandparents and uncles and aunties, but your friends at school or maybe even the people you've met at your local sports club) can broaden your view of what your own heritage means to you, and of all the amazing cultural things like food, art, or dance and language that are associated with your incredible heritage!

The goal is to be proud of who you are and of all the things that make you, you! So that you can make even more friends and connections without feeling you have to change yourself to fit in. (That's a common feeling – I can definitely relate!)

Being a little bit different from our friends can sometimes feel awkward. I know what it feels like to be seen as the odd one out – you might remember that I mentioned that I am the only mixed Black girl in my family – and sure, sometimes, especially when I was younger, I just wanted to blend in and not be noticed.

or called out for being different. But now . . . **now I RELISH IT**.

> ***My superpower is that I am unique.***

I know that sounds a little cheesy, but I really mean it. I love looking different, I love standing out in a crowd, I love wearing my Afro as big as I can get it, and I even love the idea that when people see me they often want to come and talk to me. They want to ask me questions about my family, or about my heritage, about whether I've been to Jamaica, or about why I look different. When I was younger I would dread these questions – but now, funnily enough, I often think about how I'll never be lonely and I'll never be short of an interesting conversation.

Because I've spent a lot of time getting to know myself and others who are mixed, I feel like I have both the confidence to express myself if someone makes me uncomfortable in one of these interactions, but also to share my knowledge so we can all have a better understanding and appreciation of other cultures, their histories and stories.

So this chapter is all about digging deeper to discover whether things that may have previously made you feel as though you stand out in a negative way (perhaps something that has made you feel embarrassed or nervous at times?) might ACTUALLY be really beautiful. How these things make you unique in a really amazing way. Hopefully, this in turn will help you celebrate yourself.

And maybe, just maybe, once you discover more about yourself through the exploration we are about to do, you'll want to talk about all these things that make you who you are. And this in turn will help you to make **even more** connections to people who are both similar to you and also very different.

Let's find out how.

All the ways we can make positive connections

I'll let you in on a secret. I've found that the more positive connections I make, and the more people I speak to about being mixed – their experiences, where their parents are from, where they grew up, what languages they do or don't speak, what foods they grew up eating and whether they look similar to their siblings – the more I learn. And the happier I become. Because I feel like I am part of a bigger group, and I start to feel a real sense of belonging. And it doesn't matter whether the people I make these connections with have similar experiences to my own, or completely different ones.

I want that for every single one of you reading this.

I know it can be scary sometimes to admit to ourselves that we don't know as much about something as we wish we did, or as much as people expect us to based on the way we look or the way they perceive us. It can prevent us from sharing or talking about who we are, but learning more about yourself, your heritage and your identity, especially the parts that you didn't already know, will feel way less daunting once you have a plan! Trust me.

Over the years, I have actually found lots of ways to explore heritage and identity that I have really enjoyed. Hopefully, you will find something that appeals to you – it could be anything. Maybe you'll be inspired by something you already like that's linked to one of your cultures. One of my friends, Yuri Davis, who is a fashion designer, is mixed Jamaican and Japanese, and she found herself incredibly inspired when she started learning about Manga and about Japanese female motorbike riders (she tells me it's a big thing in Japanese movies!).

Yuri was so interested in researching these things that she ended up designing collections of clothes around them, while taking the opportunity to learn about her heritage and herself at the same time. She told me that weaving these themes into her designs made her feel closer to her Japanese ancestry. If we learn more about something and include it in things we do every day, like our work, we begin to feel like it's part of us and that no one can take it away or dismiss it . . .

Food

I don't know about you but I **LOVE** to eat. I've always been a bit of a foodie. According to my parents, I loved tasting different, wonderful things that people don't expect young children to like. I've always loved things like olives, curry, anchovies, blue cheese, okra, and for a treat, a raw piece of lemon . . . People say most of these foods are supposed to be something you either grow into or you hate, but lots of people find the taste or the texture of these foods too much!

Anyway, if you're still reading and I haven't completely lost you, I have always really liked experimenting with foods and I am never happier than when I'm yamming

> **EXERCISE NO.7**

- **Do you like to try different foods, or do you prefer to play it safe?**

- **What are your three favourite things to eat? Are they similar or completely different?**

- **Do you know in which countries any of the ingredients in your favourite meals are most commonly grown? Write the ingredients down in a list and see if you know where they might come from.**

- **What foods did your parents grow up eating? Do they cook the same things for you?**

- **Do you ever cook meals with your parents? If so, what do you make?**

down on a good meal. I love to try different types of foods from different places. I like variety, and I find a plate of rice and peas and brown stew chicken just as delicious as a spag bol (which was something my mum used to cook a lot), or a plate of my Nene's (my mum-in-law) jollof rice (Nigerian jollof of course).

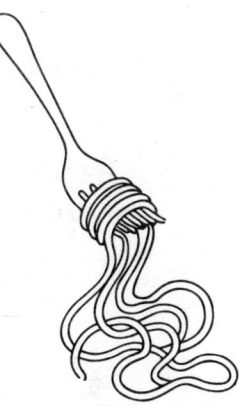

The reason I asked you to do that little exercise is because I wanted to get you thinking about food and the way it makes us feel. How it reminds us of moments, or people, or smells, how it comforts us and reminds us of home. Food actually, if you think about it, packs a powerful punch when it comes to the part it can play in our lives, the memories we can make when we are eating it and the things we can learn from it, especially when it comes to our identities.

Recently, when I visited Jamaica, I learnt about three new fruits that I didn't even know existed:

1. Soursop – which is soft and white under its skin, and its flesh tastes sour (as the name gives away!).

2. Ginep – a very small green ball of a fruit, which tastes a bit like a sweet-and-sour, boiled sweet but also a bit like a lychee. Delicious and moorish. To eat them you peel off the skin and suck the fruit off of the pip in the middle.

3. Acerola or Jamaica Cherry – these are smaller and look more like a berry than the ones commonly found in the UK, and they taste tart and sweet.

When I was there, I learnt how to cook the national dish, Ackee and Saltfish, which I had tasted before but had never cooked. Ackee has soft yellow flesh which, when it is cooked, looks a little like scrambled egg and tastes **sooo** yummy with a side of fried plantain (which is a fruit from the banana family).

Now when I think of those fruits I immediately think of Jamaica, and when I want to feel closer to that part of my heritage I can cook the meal I want to eat myself. It's comforting to be able to do that. Food is something we can really take ownership over learning about, and we can also teach other family members the recipes we learn.

> ***It's something we can take with us wherever we are in the world.***

A friend of mine, Anna Sulan, who writes a lot about food, history and identity, also explained to me how we can chart the journey of a people and tell their story through the foods they might traditionally cook. We can literally see where our ancestors have been from the foods they have eaten and the ingredients that are commonly used in their meals, by looking into where those ingredients grow. For example, with the Chinese Haka people, their food dishes tell us a lot about how their ancestors became nomads when they were forced off their own land and about how they had to learn to forage and make something out of very little.

Another friend of mine, also called Ana (you have to be called Anna to be my friend) told me that she learnt how to cook a special cuisine which is a fusion of Portuguese and Chinese food, precisely because she wanted to find a way to connect with her mixed-race identity. She is from a place called Macau, which is a Chinese province that was formerly a colony of Portugal, and her mum is Portuguese while her dad is Chinese. She told me that when she decided she wanted to get close to her Macanese heritage, she first thought about learning the Macanese language. But then she found out it was what people call a 'dying language' – meaning very, very few people speak it any more, making it really difficult to learn. When she realized this, she thought about how food might be a good gateway to feeling more connected to her Macanese culture, which is a mix of Chinese and Portuguese culture.

She started to learn to cook the recipes for the food she had eaten growing up in Macau – like **Minchi**, which is a delicious dish of mincemeat, potato and onions heavily flavoured with soy sauce, spices, like cumin, and garlic. It is served with a fried egg.

Once she learnt to cook these dishes, she decided she wanted to share them with people. Macanese is a little-known cuisine, a fusion or mixture of Portuguese and Chinese tastes, so she made it her mission to bring it to the world. Ana is now known for having created the first Macanese pop-up restaurant in London and she regularly puts on supper clubs – big dinner events – where other people can come and taste the cuisine of her childhood and her heritage.

Through this journey with food, she has met lots of other people. People searching for a taste of home, who may not have previously been able to find the dishes that feel familiar and comforting, and also people who are just interested to learn more about Macanese cooking and food.

On the next page is an example of a recipe that is a little bit of a heritage exploration from Chef Melissa Hemsley, who also tells us a little bit about her background, why she likes to cook so much and how she's grown to love Filipino food and her mum's cooking over time.

EXERCISE NO.8

RECIPE WRITING, COLLECTING AND COOKING

Try this exercise if you think food might be your chosen way to positively connect.

Design a recipe that combines ingredients from your different cultures or heritage groups.

Melissa Hemsley is a self-taught chef, best-selling cookbook author, real food activist and sustainability champion.

Dear Reader,

My name is Melissa, and my father is from the UK while my mother is from the Philippines. I grew up in the suburbs of London, and my school at the time was predominately white, and, I'm sad to say, I didn't like my mum cooking Filipino food when my friends came over. I was even shy about the smell of our food. All the garlic, soy, ginger, chilli and fish sauce! Sometimes mackerel for breakfast. It felt so different from my friends' homes with 'normal smells' like cupcakes baking, oven chips and beans on toast.

I turn forty years old this year, which means I'm now most definitely a grown-up, but whenever I'm around my mother I still feel like a teenager, maybe because she still tells me off!?

I wonder if I'll be like that in the future . . . I am mum

to a two-year-old girl, whom we named Summer as she was born around the summer solstice – the longest day of the year due to the sun setting later than any other evening in 365 days.

It's a bit of an unusual name. When I was younger, I wanted to be anything other than different, and if you'd asked me when I was a teenager if I'd give my future child an unusual name, I'd have said NO WAY! Don't give your child a reason to feel different! But now I know the truth . . . it's our infinite differences that

makes every one of us beautifully special. And I wish I'd known this when I was growing up. And now I'm responsible for someone else's home smell!

People often say my daughter looks like my mum which my mum obviously loves. Things I'd shy away from as a child, I positively nag my mum to do for my daughter. I keep reminding her to please speak Tagalog to my daughter (the official language of the Philippines) as she didn't speak it to me growing up, which I feel sad about as it sort of feels like a lost connection with my heritage. My Filipino cousins tease me that I only know the swear words and how to say *I'm hungry!*

> **Gutom na ako**

My job these days is as a cookbook author, and I share free recipes for busy families on social media. I'm halfway through a degree in nutrition as I'd love to support people to feel their best through food and lifestyle. It's never too late to learn or change career so I hope you don't feel the pressure to have it all worked out now. There's time to explore so many avenues. And studying as an adult feels so different from studying sitting on a school chair.

I like to cook and eat food from all across the world – some of my favourite cuisines are Vietnamese, Thai, Kenyan, Cambodian, Japanese, Moroccan, Syrian, Palestinian and of course Filipino.

I started cooking for bands and actors as a private chef for over fifteen years. They wanted me to cook them food that helps them feel strong, energetic and healthy and feel good inside and out. I've never cooked for artists like Olivia Rodrigo, Hailee Steinfeld and Bruno Mars but was thrilled to find out that, like me, they have Filipino heritage.

I love feeding people, and I definitely get that from my mum as Filipinos are known for being great cooks and generous feeders. One of my most vivid memories as a child is every Friday my mum would make me turn off the TV and have me on doorbell duty to open the front door for many, many arriving aunties (any female older than me!).

I would help them with their pots and pans, still warm, that they carried off the bus or from the car boot and then we'd eat a huge communal feast, after they'd all pray together and then everyone would take leftovers home. There would always be extras on purpose. My British friends laugh that I like to send them home with leftovers which they aren't as used to! I also adore traditional British food and my mum is great at that too – she is excellent at roast dinners, shepherd's pies etc., but when I thought about sharing a recipe with you, I knew it had to be something I adored as a child and make weekly now too. It's called pancit, and I always think of it as party noodles as you'll always see a vat of pancit at a family get-together (a fiesta, I grew up going to huge fiestas in London parks with traditional Filipino dancing, BBQs, parades and karaoke).

Here's the recipe for pancit party noodles. There are so many different versions of it – there are 7,000 islands in the Philippines so every region has their own version. You can add shredded chicken or pork or little shrimp but it's delicious with veggies, too. Work out how you like it best!

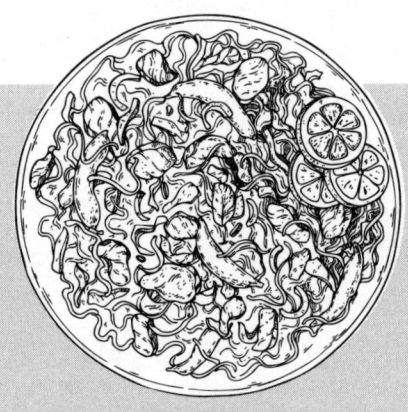

PANCIT NOODLES

Serves 4 as a main or 8 as a side, takes 20 minutes

Ingredients

250g noodles (I like vermicelli)

3 tbsp olive oil, coconut oil or ghee

1 large onion, finely sliced

6 cloves of garlic, finely chopped

3 carrots, julienned (finely sliced)

1 sweetheart cabbage, finely shredded

3 large handfuls of green beans (about 300g), halved

200ml stock/broth/water

3 tbsp soy sauce, to taste

1 tbsp fish sauce, optional
Juice of a lime or ½ lemon
Chilli flakes
Salt and pepper to taste
To serve
1 lime or lemon, in wedges
1 small bunch of spring onions, finely sliced

Method
1. Cook noodles according to packet instructions, then rinse and drain, leave to cool, toss in a little oil to stop them sticking. Top tip for soba noodles: cook them in plenty of water and use forks to separate the noodles for the first 2 minutes of cooking.
2. Fry the onions in oil/ghee for 5–7 minutes, stirring from time to time, until softened (I use the same pan to cook the noodles, ideally a large deep-sided pan).
3. Add the garlic and a big pinch of sea salt and fry for another minute.
4. Add the green beans to the pan and stir fry for 2–3 minutes, add a splash of water/stock/broth if needed to stop it sticking and cook until starting to soften.
5. Add the carrots and cabbage for a final 2 minutes until the veg is just tender.
6. Add soy sauce, fish sauce (if using), chilli flakes, lemon or lime juice, stir then add noodles, a few handfuls at a time can make it easier and toss the noodles through the veg. Season to taste and serve with spring onions and lime or lemon wedges.

EXERCISE NO.9

Design your own recipe that takes inspiration from a combination of two or more of your cultures or heritage. You can ask an elder, your mum, dad, uncle or aunty to help with this if you want to. Or, there are plenty of resources and chefs online who might give you inspiration!

It doesn't need to be complicated. It can be simple just like Melissa's Pancit Noodles

You can use Melissa's recipe above for guidance. For this task you'll need to write down all the ingredients you'll need, their quantities and then a step-by-step process of how to make the recipe!

If you need somewhere to start you might want to find out what the national dish is of each of the countries or cultures you'd like to include. For example, if I was going to make a recipe that represents my mixed heritage, the first ingredients I would start to think about would be:

1. **Ackee** – the key ingredient of Jamaica's national dish

2. **Crumpets** – while these are not a national dish, they are widely enjoyed across the country (fun fact: because Britain is seen as having multiculturalism at the heart of its history, there is no official national dish).

Next you might like to research how those foods are usually cooked. Then I think it would be fun to put your own spin on it!

One of the things that I've discovered from talking to friends is that – even though our parents or grandparents might have grown up far apart, on other sides of the world – the foods they include, or the way they cook them, can be similar. And so can their approach to sitting down for meals and what mealtimes look like.

Creativity and inspiration

There are plenty of mixed-race artists, creatives, singers and sports stars that in some way use their experiences of being mixed race as inspiration for their art just like my friend Yuri. Often this process helps them feel happier in their identity.

Olivia Dean used her mixed-race heritage and her Jamaican grandma, who came to the UK as part of the **Windrush** generation as the inspiration to her song 'Carmen'. She talks about how her grandma's bravery in migrating from Guyana to the UK, and surviving racism and hardship, inspired her art. The song celebrates Olivia's grandma's strength and bravery, and uses steel pans (a traditional Caribbean instrument) to show her pride in her culture and history. I think it's very cool that Olivia was able to learn about her grandma's culture and claim it as part of her own, sharing it with the world in her song.

QUICK DICTIONARY PULL-OUT

WINDRUSH

The *Empire Windrush* was a huge ship that came to Britain in 1948. On it were people from Caribbean countries like Jamaica, Trinidad and Barbados. They came to help rebuild Britain after the Second World War, because there weren't enough workers across areas like nursing, bus driving, teaching and building.

Griff is a pop musician and singer who has Vietnamese and Jamaican parents. She is famous for songs like 'Miss Me', which explores the topic of identity and previous versions of yourself. She has spoken about how her mixed Vietnamese and Jamaican background makes her unique in a very cool way, and about how it influences her work through her mixed and eclectic music tastes. This has helped her craft a distinctive sound, but also helped her be comfortable with an image that is totally different from other musicians. She said she is used to people thinking she looks unconventional and that helps her experiment. 'It's allowed me to be more comfortable with looking different and being bolder, fashion-wise,' Griff says.

Charlotte Edey is a mixed Caribbean and British artist who uses her art to explore her sense of self, painting figures with big Afros into all of her paintings. They float in worlds that look beautiful but also a little bit alien, like they are not on Earth. I remember the first time I saw one of her paintings I was taken aback by how much I felt like I was seeing a little piece of myself in them reflected back at me. I had rarely ever seen women, or people who looked like me, depicted in art like this, so it was surprising and really cool! Charlotte said that she felt the same way, which was why she painted them that way.

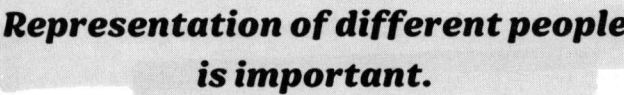

Representation of different people is important.

When I was growing up, I didn't see a lot of imagery, drawings, designs or people on TV that looked like me, and now that I do see more it makes me proud. When we don't see representations of ourselves very often it can make us feel a bit unseen or even unwelcome in certain places, so seeing people who look like you can be really empowering.

Actor, author and singer Jordan Stephens (from a band called Rizzle Kicks) and designer Beth Suzanna have turned their own experiences of being mixed into a children's book called *The Missing Piece* – it's a beautiful story of a little girl who is trying to complete a puzzle but she can't because one piece is missing. The puzzle is a metaphor for her and how she feels about her identity.

Other art and creative projects to look out for:

YouTube
Jassa Ahluwalia – Both Not Half TEDx
Kids of the Colony
The Mixed Museum

Social Media Community
Halu Halo
Mixed Race Faces
Mixed Up podcast

Poetry
Dean Atta – I Come From

Books
Dean Atta – The Black Flamingo
Confetti: Poems for Children by Pat Mora
The Other Half of My Heart by Sundee T. Frazier
Flying the Dragon by Natalie Dias Lorenzi

Half and Half by Lensey Namioka
Transcendent by Patrick Gallagher
Birdie by J. P. Rose
Fable House by E. L. Norry
My Life as a Chameleon by Diana Anyakwo
The Weight of Blood by Tiffany D. Jackson
Dread Nation by Justina Ireland
Tsunami Girl by Julian Sedgwick
(S)kin by Ibi Zoboi
The House at the Edge of the World by Nadine Aisha Jassat

TV & Film
Shadow and Bone
K-Pop Demon Hunters

6
Language and Belonging

Ryan Alexander Holmes

is an actor and content creator based in Los Angeles. He's known for his social media presence where he uses comedy and writing to explore and embrace his mixed Chinese and African American heritage.

Dear Reader,

Language isn't just about communication, it's about connection. It's how us humans carry memories, culture, and identity across generations. For those of us who are mixed, simultaneously inhabiting the intersection of multiple cultures, language can feel like a bridge to something we've never known but is deep within our blood.

As a kid, I went to Chinese school on weekends, while my friends were having fun doing literally anything else. And at the time, I felt like a prisoner being forced to memorize symbols I had no connection to. I didn't fully appreciate it. Not yet.

In college, I decided to study Mandarin again. This time not because someone told me to, but because I wanted to. I wanted to speak to my grandma 外婆 (wài pó) in her language. She raised my mom, who raised me, and yet for most of my life, I couldn't fully understand her stories, her humor, her love. Once I started learning, everything changed. Suddenly, I had access, not just to her words, but to our shared history. To the games she played as a kid. To the strength it took for her to survive wars and cross continents. To the way she sees the world.

That connection gave me more of me. It helped me feel whole.

And I'm still learning. The process never really stops and neither does the discovery or the joy. Each new word, each new conversation, each awkward moment I fumble through, it's all part of getting closer, to her, to my heritage, to myself.

Language, like identity, isn't always easy. But what I've learned, and what Jassa has learned, is that it's always worth it. Because on the other side of effort is belonging. And that kind of belonging doesn't come from other people's approval or validation. It comes from knowing where you come from and being proud of it, no matter the language.

Ryan

Language

Language can be a bit of a slippery character. If you're learning a language at school you might agree that it takes lots of hours of work to feel like you've got something concrete out of it.

When you learn that 40 per cent of the world's population (almost half of us) only speak one language, only three per cent of people around the world can speak over four languages and less than one per cent of people worldwide speak five or more languages, it's no surprise that it's hard to learn a language.

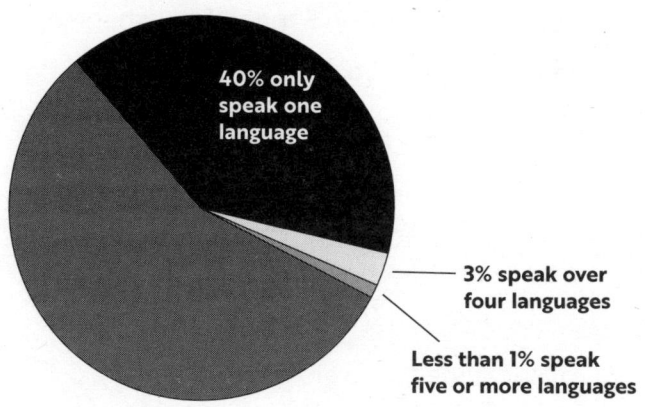

But! When I spoke to some of my friends, like Ryan Alexander Holmes who is Chinese and African American and Jassa Ahluwalia who is mixed Punjabi and white British (and whom we met on page 82), I have changed my mind on whether the lemon juice is worth the squeeze. Both Ryan and Jassa are great examples of people who have gained so much from learning the language of one of their heritages.

For Ryan, it enables him to communicate in Chinese with his grandma or his 外婆 (wài pó). If he hadn't learnt Chinese they wouldn't be able to talk to each other, because she doesn't speak English – Mandarin is her only language. So you can imagine the joy he gets from this – now they are basically besties and very cute to see together. Because Ryan has learnt the language, his wai pó can also tell him about her time growing up in China and teach him how to play Chinese games like mahjong. She's shared her experience of surviving two wars and travelling from Taipei to Shanghai, then on to America.

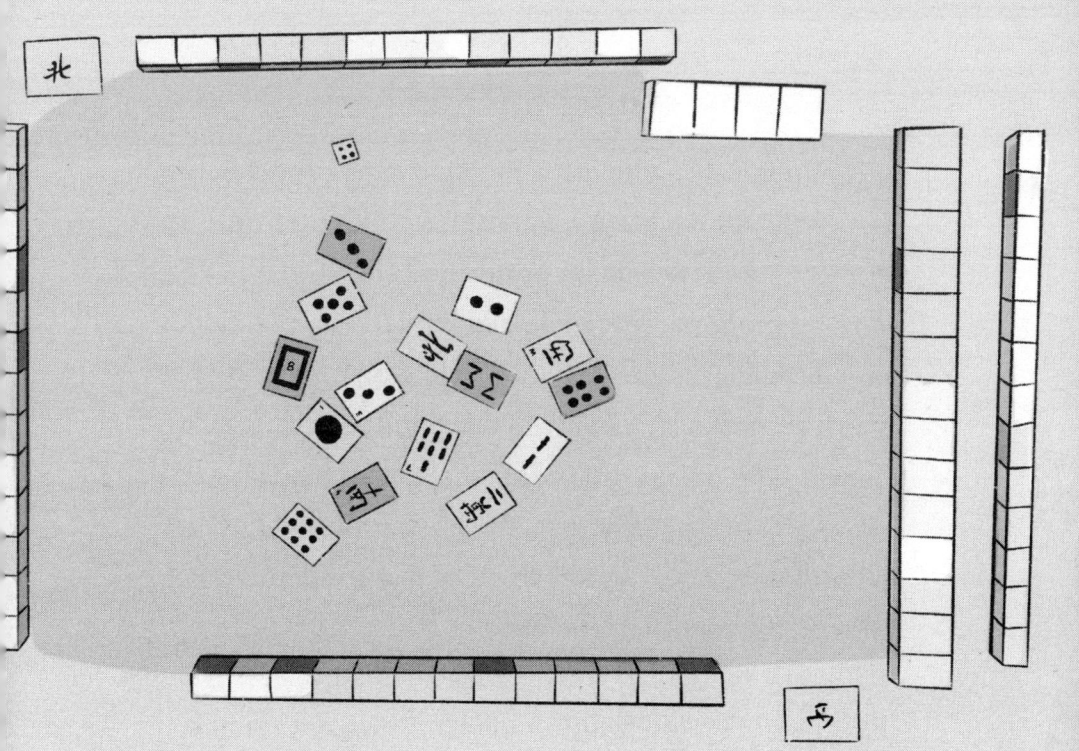

Ryan has said before that although he is not encouraged to learn this language out of a feeling of missing something, he does see it as an opportunity to get closer to his grandma, his heritage and history. All of this has helped him to get to know himself better. When he speaks his language, he speaks it with so much pride!

Jassa, who is mixed Punjabi and white British, lives in the United Kingdom and has spent a lot of time learning Punjabi. He now speaks it fluently. His accent and intonation (I am told) are absolutely pitch perfect. Jassa grew up in Leicester with a British mother and a Punjabi father, where he spent much of his childhood with his Punjabi grandparents. At home, he spoke English, but with his grandparents he spoke Punjabi. This helped him learn his language from a young age. He also often spent summers in India with his grandparents and so he was able to be right in the heart of all the things he now loves about Punjabi culture – the vibrant colours and dancing, the fragrant smell of Indian spices, the welcoming nature of the people, and of course, the sing-song melody of the language. Jassa believes that his language is his guide to his identity, his heritage and his place in the world. Just like a compass that helps you to find your direction, Punjabi helps him stay connected to his roots and his community, and also to make sense of his mixed identity as both British and Punjabi.

Now the thing about Jassa is that his skin is very pale and often, on first glance, people mistake him for being a white British man. We talked about this in chapter three – this is called being **misidentified**.

Sometimes when people realize that Jassa is mixed, they might use the phrase **'white passing'** to describe him. 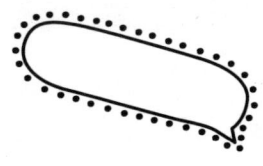 When they say this, they mean he is someone who could easily be in a room with other white people and with them thinking of him as a white man, if he never said otherwise.

Privilege that comes with being mistaken for a white person.

Because of the way Jassa looks, and because he is often perceived to be white, he is treated differently in different situations. For example, if someone does think he is a white man, he might be more likely to get a job or be paid more, or it might be as simple as the idea that he doesn't face racism in his everyday life.

EXERCISE NO.10

BUT WHAT DO MIXED-RACE PEOPLE LOOK LIKE ANYWAY?

With this exercise I want you to think a little about other mixed people you know, what they look like and also what you look like. And then I want you to think about how we are portrayed in the films, books and TV you have read or seen.

Get a pen and some paper and jot down your answers.

Now that's done, I want you to reflect on the differences between the ways mixed people you know look, and the way mixed people you see in the media look. We can use Ryan and Jassa as our first examples – Jassa has pale skin, light brown hair and dark brown eyes. He is often mistaken for being white. Ryan has brown skin, an Afro and oval eyes. He says that people always tell him he doesn't 'look Chinese' and he responds that they 'just haven't met a Chinese person who looks like him'.

The point of this exercise is to demonstrate that mixed people look vastly different. We come in so many different shapes, heights and sizes and from all over the globe. There is no one way to look as a mixed person, and although other people might have their own ideas about what they think the way you look says about you, it really shouldn't make a difference to how you feel about yourself and the identity you are growing into.

On the other hand, I do think Jassa has found being misidentified by other Punjabi people a bit hurtful or upsetting at times. As we've talked about, it can be painful not to be recognized or accepted by people who share your heritage.

Jassa says that when he does speak Punjabi, he is praised by other Punjabis, which feels good, but it also gives him a sense of identity that no one can alter or take away from him.

So even if it's just a few words and phrases you can

get started with, it's worth looking into learning one of your cultural languages. Jassa tells me that learning his language was like accessing a whole new world that you wouldn't be able to understand without it, because some of the words don't even exist in English! How cool is that?!

One example he gives is **'Sanjog'** (ਸੰਜੋਗ), which refers to a meaningful connection or destiny, often seen as events aligning in a way that feels like fate, but there really isn't an equivalent word in the English language.

Journaling and letter writing

Letter writing is another great way to create positive connections. I find this particularly useful as a reminder of what I am learning about myself as I go along. Sometimes, I simply write a letter to myself so that I can open it up and read it again in a year's time. It helps me to look back and see what I was worried about, whether I was confused or frustrated with some aspect of my identity, what I wanted to learn about myself and my family, and to see if I've managed to do those things.

EXERCISE NO.11

Using the following prompts – write a letter to either:
- **yourself**
- **a friend**
- **someone you admire**
- **a family member you feel safe with**

Write them a letter about:

1. How you feel about being mixed after reading some of this book.
2. Things you still have questions about. These could be questions about your family heritage or history, the countries your grandparents are from, customs and traditions from one of your parents, language or foods. It could be simply about how to do your hair, or why you look a little different from your parents or your siblings (if you do). Or it might be a more difficult question around things people have said to you that have felt unkind.
3. Things you have learnt about yourself.
4. The things you are proud of when you think about being mixed. For example, I am proud of the fact that being mixed means I am open to hearing and being considerate to other people's views or beliefs

when they are very different from my own. I think my ability to do this is linked to being made up of different cultures. Being mixed has encouraged me to explore other people's cultures and their history.

Now fold up your letter. If it's for you, hide it away and ask someone to remind you to open it in a year's time. If you wrote it for a family member, you can share it with them or read it to them if you feel safe enough to do so.

Reading

What you're doing at this moment – although it might not seem like it immediately, especially if you're literally by yourself, reading alone – believe it or not, is part of connecting with others. You're actually connecting with me right now. You're also connecting with the author of the letter at the beginning of this chapter and all of the other letter writers. You already know a little bit of their stories and you may be able to see how their stories connect to your own or is a mirror to your own story in some way. Hopefully reading this book may even inspire you to reach out to people that may be able to tell you about their own experiences, which you might share with them.

Don't stay quiet — keep talking

The most important thing is to keep talking about what your mixed-race identity means to you.

Keep discussing how it feels to be a member of part of more than one group at the same time. Think and talk about whether you prefer to balance your identities at the same time, or whether you sometimes prefer to choose one over the other, and why. This might change over time and that's totally normal and absolutely fine.

Find ways to talk to your parents and your friends about the positive things you've found out about mixed experiences, both your own and other people's, and how you connect to it whether that be through art, or music or language or journaling.

Keep talking!

7
Identity Fluidity

Asia Jackson

is an actress, speaker, and content creator. Her work explores beauty, fashion and culture through the lens of identity.

Dear Identity Explorer,

Growing up mixed, people often expected me to pick a side. And when I didn't, they tried to pick one for me.

If I said, 'I'm Black' people assumed I was rejecting my Asian side. If I said, 'I'm Asian' they thought I was ignoring the fact that I'm also Black. But that's never how identity has worked for me. When I say I'm Black, I'm still Asian. When I say I'm Asian, I'm still Black. I've never stopped being both at the same time.

I don't exist in separate halves — I exist in full.

I'm not Either/Or. I'm Both/And. I am African American and Indigenous Filipino. I am Louisiana Creole and Ibaloi. And all of those things live in me, together.

It took me a long time to understand that I don't owe anyone an explanation that makes them comfortable.

Simply calling myself 'mixed' doesn't capture the full truth of who I am. Yes, it's part of my identity – but not the whole of it. 'Mixed' is just an adjective. It could mean anything. But I'm specifically Black and Filipino. I am shaped by my cultures, my family and my history. And that specificity is powerful. That's where the beauty lies.

So if you've ever felt like you had to choose, or like your identity was 'too complicated', know this: your story is allowed to be layered. **You're allowed to be BOTH. You're allowed to be ALL.**

With love,

Asia Jackson ♡

Identity Fluidity
What's that?

This chapter is all about thinking differently about the way people see race and identity. Rather than seeing our identity as being rigid and fixed, like a painting that is completely finished and has been glazed and hung in the museum, we are going to look at identity like a work still in progress, always changing. Imagine a painting that sits in your studio and that is just for you, to which you can keep painting new layers and colours on for as long as you like. You might want to add new bits to it, and the painting may grow and change over time, but it's still **YOUR** painting. You get to decide where to take it next. This is exactly the way in which we are going to think about being open to the idea of identity changing for us, and this feels especially important when it comes to mixed people.

The way I would describe identity for a mixed person is like a journey on a raft, heading down a river that could go on for the entirety of your life. You might think that travelling downstream is right for you at some point, and at another you might feel you want to travel back the

other way. And that's fine. It's not out of the ordinary at all.

You see, for mixed-race people identity can be far more of a fluid thing. What's more, our identity, how we describe ourselves, or which groups we feel more of an affinity towards might change over time. These things might even change quite **a lot** over the course of our lives.

In this chapter I want us to get comfortable with the idea of:

'For now' and 'Both/And'

Having spoken to a lot of mixed people on my podcast *Mixed Up*, I can see that a lot of people who are mixed (including me) go through a number of steps in their identity journey.

➡ 1) The first step might be not thinking about race, ethnicity and heritage at all. And just living without considering it. Especially when we are younger, we get most of our ideas about who we are from our parents, so everything seems simpler and it's only when we go out into the world, to school, or clubs or jobs, and we come into close contact with people outside of our families that we realize what other people think of us does affect us. As we were talking about when we discussed Jassa's experience, it often feels like it matters whether people include us in their groups or not. How other people react to us can add or take away from our sense of self if we allow it to.

 2) The second stage might be thinking a bit more about your race, ethnicity and heritage, or the groups you feel you belong in, or don't belong in, but it's OK not having all the answers. You might just be beginning to start to search for connections or investigate your heritage by asking your family questions or reading books like Dean mentioned right at the beginning of the book. At this stage, we might start wondering about family members we don't know or places connected to our ancestry that we've never visited. You might

want to visit those places and learn more about the tribes or cultures that are in your ancestry. Like Asia, you might begin to feel strongly that the history of these groups is really important to you.

Asia says in her letter, **'I am African American and Indigenous Filipino. I am Louisiana Creole and Ibaloi. And all of those things live in me, together.'**

And I know from a conversation we had on my podcast that she's learnt a lot about her Filipino heritage during her life – she told me some of the things she knows and that she's proud of when it comes to being **Ibaloi**.

Ibaloi people and culture

The Ibaloi are often called **'people of the mountains'**, because they live high up in the cool, green Cordillera Mountains. The **Ibaloi** (sometimes spelled Ibaloy or Nabaloi) are an **Indigenous group of people from the Philippines**. They mostly live in the **mountains of Benguet province**, in the northern part of the country (the Cordillera region). They are **farmers** who grow rice, root crops, and vegetables on terraces carved into the hillsides and they are known for their **music, dance, and storytelling**, especially during gatherings called cañao which are big feasts where the community come together.

But Asia makes a point of acknowledging that just because she may be more interested in one side of her heritage at one time in her life than another doesn't

mean that she thinks of herself as anything other than whole. She is Filipino **AND** she is Black **AND** she is mixed.

3) And the third stage may come a lot later. It may or may not be feeling like you are safe and secure and sure of your identity. This might take a long time, or a lifetime, or your feeling around this might keep changing, and that's also fine.

Other mixed people say that their journey with identity looked more like:

1) Not feeling connected to any particular group and feeling quite alone, or feeling sure of their individual identity that has nothing to do with a group.

2) Then maybe one day they pick a group that is aligned to one of their cultural or racial backgrounds and they begin to express aspects of their identity that are the same or similar to this group.

3) Sometimes people then feel a bit guilty because they sort of forgot about their other racial/cultural groups, or pushed them to the back of their mind so they could fit in.

 4) Eventually after the journey we've been talking about in this book they begin to feel comfortable and free to express both, or all sides of their ethnic and cultural identities.

Everyone's journey is different and even if yours doesn't look like any of those I mentioned – that's also fine.

Although it is your choice and prerogative to decide on your own identity journey and how you express it, people might mistake your actions while you are exploring your identity for **'cultural appropriation'** or they might say you are **code switching**.

PREROGATIVE: A power or right that only you have.

QUICK DICTIONARY PULL-OUT
CULTURAL APPROPRIATION

This is where someone takes on, imitates or adopts elements of another culture that they don't belong to. This is a bit like borrowing something that you can benefit from without asking, and not fully appreciating and understanding its meaning and why it is special to that person or group.

QUICK DICTIONARY PULL-OUT
CODE SWITCHING

When somebody changes their accent, tone of voice, mannerisms or behaviours depending on where they are and who they're with, so they can fit in with the people. It is a form of mirroring. Most people do a bit of this – behaving differently at school with their friends than with their parents at home – but we call it Code Switching when the change in behaviour is in order to fit in with a particular group. People often talk about people of colour code switching in order to be able to succeed in white environments at work, for example. But it's a problem because it stems from people feeling like they have to hide who they are.

What should you do if someone accuses you of this?

The short answer: it's complicated. Because often people who are upset or sensitive to the idea of their cultural identity being mimicked or mirrored by someone who they don't consider to be part of their group will have good reason to feel this way. This may be because aspects of their cultural identity or the way they look have been culturally appropriated before for the purpose of making money. This is a form of what we call cultural appropriation because it is where a more privileged group can benefit off the things that make up another group's identity – things which the original group cannot benefit from.

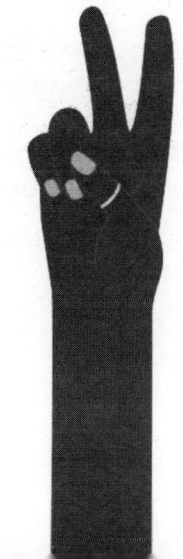

Back to what you should do if someone accuses you of this

Well, let's start by reminding ourselves that it's natural to want to try out different ways to express different parts of your identity. And as long as you make sure to do your research so you can have the best understanding of your cultures, then you should be able to confidently tell whoever is accusing you that you are, for example, Nigerian AND Filipino, and so it's comfortable for you to wear your hair in braids and wear ankara cloth and you're proud to represent one of your cultures in this way whenever you get the opportunity.

And just because you want to represent your Nigerian culture and perhaps talk more about it one day, and you might want to represent your Filipino culture at another time, that doesn't make either one less important or valid than the other.

You can practise the 'And/Both' Statement and the 'For Now' Statement with your parents.

EXERCISE NO.12

Write a statement about who you are, talking about one or more of your identities. You can include the food you like eating, some of the books you like, your hobbies, and other things that might connect you to one or more of your cultures.

Repeat this exercise every week, and see how it changes. Remember that it's totally fine for you to feel differently about different parts of your identity each day.

Example: My name is **Emma** and I am BOTH Black AND mixed-race.
Example: I am **Ryan** and I am BOTH Chinese AND Black.
Example: I am **Jassa** and I am BOTH Punjabi AND British.
Example: I am **Yuri** and I am BOTH Japanese AND Black Jamaican, AND I'm mixed.

Example: My name is **Emma** and FOR NOW I'm really enjoying exploring my Jamaican heritage.

Example: I am **Ayesha**. I am mixed Bangladeshi AND Chinese and FOR NOW most of my friends are Bangladeshi AND my favourite hobby is learning to play the Ektara (a string instrument that is popular in my culture) but next year I want to learn to play mahjong with my Chinese mum.

8
You Decide — The Self-Affirmation

Jessie Mei Li

was born to an English mother and Chinese father. They have spoken out about how little there is positive East Asian and biracial representation on-screen.

Dear Reader,

I'm Jessie Mei Li,

And I'm so pleased to be able to write to you.

Growing up mixed-race is pretty confusing. For some of us it's a blessing, the idea of being welcome in more than one culture. But we can also feel lost – I know I did when I was younger. I never felt 'enough' of anything.

I'm mixed Chinese and English, and I grew up in a town where families like mine were not so common. To all my non-Chinese friends, I was 'the Asian one' and wore this with pride, answering friends' questions about my culture and defending my family fiercely from racist remarks.

But I also remember feeling awkward and embarrassed when I'd spend time with Chinese family who commented on my Western features and were disappointed that I couldn't fluently speak the language. It made me feel like an imposter. It didn't help either that my parents were divorced; I felt divided in two by my broken home, both sides of my life torn apart – half the time Asian, half the time white. I didn't really know where I belonged or whose side I was on.

Sometimes I felt lonely . . . never truly happy . . . always misunderstood . . .

But it was my need to be understood for who I really was, not who I was expected to be, that lead to the most meaningful friendships in my life – I wanted to be accepted as just 'me', so I always accepted others for who they truly were too. Now, I have such wonderful, vibrant people around me from all different backgrounds, many who never felt like they 'belonged' either. And I realized – we all belong together. Being with people who love you for who you are, in places or cultures that you feel connected to, wherever that may be – that's where you belong. No one else gets to decide for you, or label you, or say you don't measure up to how you 'should' be. People who think that way often just have a thing or two to learn about the world.

The best thing I learnt? You are enough because you are already Whole – a whole lot of interesting experiences, languages and stories in one unique person. Your own exciting mixture of colours and flavours and music. I hope that, like I did, as you go through life you'll see there are so many people like you who'll understand you and your experience of life, entirely and instantly. It's magical. And even if you haven't quite worked out where you belong yet, that's OK, you'll always belong to the mixed-race community. We've got each other's backs.

Jessie

You decide how you choose to identify

We've finally reached the *really* exciting part of the book.

The bit where we get to **affirm** who we are to ourselves. What I've learnt along the way is that this feels really, really good.

QUICK DICTIONARY PULL-OUT

AFFIRMATION

An affirmation is a positive sentence you say to yourself as a reminder of something good or true about who you are, or who you want to be. It's like giving yourself an uplifting and encouraging pep talk.

After you finish this chapter you may even want to do this aloud. Whenever I affirm who I am to myself, I find it's almost like that centring feeling you get when you take one really huge breath, hold it for a moment, and let it out very, very slooooooooowly. It feels both peaceful and grounding after you do it. That's how I hope this chapter feels to you.

By now, we have talked about the incredible and sometimes little-known histories of mixed-heritage people all over the world. We've probably got the jump

on our history teachers at this point (having learnt things they don't teach in the school history curriculum)!

We've talked about where we, as mixed-race people, might fit in as individuals in today's world and just how many of us there are out there, all with our different upbringings, stories and heritages. We are, after all, the fastest growing group of people in the world. And it's pretty cool to belong to such a big group, right? A group we can always say we are a part of, which gives us so many opportunities to learn – especially given how many differences there are between us – as well as similarities . . .

We've also talked about how to use those differences and similarities to make positive connections, and to support ourselves and others. You may have even used 'The Chat' chapter to help you talk to your parents about your identity. If you have, well done to you and your parents. It's not always easy to start these conversations.

So what's next? Well, we are going to take all of that reading, learning and conversation and we are going to use it to help us feel proud and sure of who we are and how we want to stand firm in communicating that to other people.

Now this next thing is very important. I want you to leave at the door all of the following:

1. Anything someone else has said you are.

2. Anything someone else has said you are not enough of.

3. Anything someone else has said that has made you feel negative, in relation to the colour of your skin or your heritage.

OK, now that we've left them behind, it's time to define ourselves just the way WE want to.

A friend of mine Asia (she wrote the letter in the last chapter – 'Identity Fluidity') once asked me how I describe myself. More specifically, she asked me how I define myself?

There is actually an important distinction between the

two things, because for me the word 'define' is about how we personally state

> *who we are rather than how we describe things like the way we look.*

How I 'define' myself can include more about how I feel and think, and how that brings meaning to who I believe I am.

This was actually the first time I've ever been asked this question in relation to being mixed-race and I had to take a moment to think about my answer.

Asia told us in her letter that she defines herself as 'Black' AND 'mixed', and that she doesn't see the descriptor of 'mixed' on its own as completely true to the way she sees herself. She went on to explain to me that as a single descriptor it doesn't feel right for

her because she thinks it's really important for her to acknowledge that she is 'Black', as it's a big part of her felt and lived identity. Asia's ethnic mix is Filipino (South East Asian) and Black – her mum is Filipino and her Dad is African American, but maybe because she considers herself appearing more Asian than Black it is important to her to assert her Blackness as part of how she identifies. This makes complete sense to me.

Asia told me that it's taken her a long time to become comfortable with who she is and how she defines herself because of racism she's faced and seen, from both inside her Filipino and African American communities and from outside of them. She's actually pretty famous on the internet for standing up against racism within the Filipino community. Historically, there has been an outdated and dangerous idea in the Philippines that people with darker skin were less beautiful than those with lighter skin. This is obviously completely untrue, but these horrible ideas come from very old historical injustices related to 'colonialization'. Asia speaks out against these ideas.

QUICK DICTIONARY PULL-OUT

COLONIZATION

Foreign nations, who were generally white, took control of territories and land that were mainly inhabited by Black and Brown peoples. Subjugation, Oppression and indoctrination around self-hatred and denigration of darker skin were all used to keep hold of control of these territories and lands. Lots of these feelings around skin tone still sadly hangs around among the communities that experienced this oppression today.

Asia created a hashtag #MagandangMorenx which means 'beautiful, brown skin' which helped to start a conversation to help people overcome these false ideas, and that's why she's kind of an internet celebrity. She's also taken a lot of time to learn about the Indigenous Filipino tribes she's descended from, and I think educating herself on the history of her Filipino people has all been very important to her in forming a confident sense of self.

What's interesting is that on that day when Asia told me she is 'Black AND she's mixed', we had been talking a lot about her Filipino heritage, and I happened to be interviewing her for my podcast *Mixed Up*, alongside my co-host Nicole Ocran. Nicole is Ghanaian and Filipino, so she also identifies 'Black' and 'mixed'. I am Jamaican and white British.

The thing we all had in common was our 'Blackness', so maybe Asia wanted to share that commonality and felt more comfortable or self-assured that day with us to say she was 'Black' AND 'mixed'. Maybe if she was with two other Filipinos she would have said, 'I am Filipino and I'm mixed.' And the point here is that that is her prerogative, her choice and her right. She is all of those things and on any given day she may feel more aligned to one of her groups than another, she may feel in certain company the need to assert one aspect of her racial identity than another. And that is **JUST FINE**.

Back to Asia's question – *How do you define yourself?*

After a bit of a pause, I responded.

I felt like I needed time to think because when she asked, I had never been asked this before and the question felt strange. No one had ever given me permission before this to describe, explain and define my own mixed identity. And in some ways I feel like Asia's confidence to describe herself this way has given me permission to state exactly who I want to be, to tell my story about myself in the way I want to.

A final activity...

One of the main things I'd like for you to take away with you after reading this book is a sense of empowerment to choose how to express your mixed-race identity. I want you to be confident in that expression, even when it changes over time.

One of the most powerful explanations of that choice that I have come across is the *Bill of Rights for People of Mixed Heritage* by Maria P. P. Root.

We can use Root's *Bill of Rights* as an affirmation and a guide to sharing who we are with others, but also to confirm our own thoughts and feelings around that to ourselves and our families who may have a desire for us to express certain aspects of our identities more than others.

As we've discussed, it can be common for our parents, friends and caregivers to want us to share their identities even though that may not be true to us. There can be lots of reasons for this, but it's important that you are the one who decides who you are.

EXERCISE NO.12

Read Root's *Bill of Rights* below. Grab a pen and some paper and write down your answers to the following questions:

- How does each statement make you feel?
- Are there any statements that you particularly agree with? What about ones that you disagree with?
- Is there anything that you would change?
- Are there are any statements that might be true for you, but different for your mum, dad, sister, brother or friend?

Bill of Rights for People of Mixed Heritage – Maria P. P. Root, author of *Racially Mixed People in America*

I HAVE THE RIGHT...

Not to justify my existence in this world. Not to keep the races separate within me. Not to justify my ethnic legitimacy.

Not to be responsible for people's discomfort with my physical or ethnic ambiguity.

I HAVE THE RIGHT...

To identify myself differently than strangers expect me to identify. To identify myself differently than how my parents identify me. To identify myself differently than my brothers and sisters. To identify myself differently in different situations.

I HAVE THE RIGHT...

To create a vocabulary to communicate about being multiracial or multiethnic. To change my identity over my lifetime––and more than once. To have loyalties and identification with more than one group of people. To freely choose whom I befriend and love.

Now, I want you to have a go at adapting the bill of rights to reflect your own experience.

I'll show you one way to write the first paragraph from my point of view:

I HAVE THE RIGHT...

Not to justify my existence in this world. Not to keep the races separate within me. Not to justify my Jamaican and British ethnic legitimacy.

Not to be responsible for people's discomfort with how I look when I am in white spaces, nor how I express myself when I am in Black spaces. I am not responsible for the awkwardness that might occur when people are not sure of my background from looking at me, or if they find me ethnically ambiguous.

I have the right to reject the policing of how I express my identity even if this comes from a family member or close friend, and certainly if it comes from a stranger.

Now it's your turn. Grab a fresh piece of paper and start copying out Root's *Bill of Rights*, adapting it to fit you and your identity as you go.

If it's too hard to write straight away, try writing down words or phrases that begin with 'I have the right . . .' and add things that help you to talk about how you would like to be free to express yourself to others about being mixed. You can flick through the book to refer to things we've talked about already if that helps.

And remember, you may want to do this once or twice a year and that's cool. You may do it once and feel really happy with your affirmation. Perhaps you'll share it with your family, or a friend, or keep it to yourself.

The main thing is that you've taken this journey of exploration and that you feel you have a path towards feeling proud, towards feeling complete, towards feeling positive about being the fully complete and rounded mixed individual that you are.

Just know, that you are enough, exactly as you are.

A final letter

Ariana Miyamoto

is a Japanese model and actress who was crowned Miss Universe Japan in 2015 — she was the first mixed-race woman to be made Miss Japan.

Dear Reader,

In 2015, I stood on a major stage for the first time – met mostly with opposition. But I kept going, embracing my true self. Now, mixed-race voices like mine are rising around the world. Our roots are not a weakness – they're our strength. Love yourself first, and love will follow.

In 2015, I stood on a major stage for the first time.

But instead of cheers, nearly 80 per cent of the voices I heard were filled with opposition.

Whenever someone dares to try something new, resistance is inevitable.

No matter how painful it is, no matter how close we come to giving up, if we learn to accept ourselves, to love ourselves, and to keep walking forward, happiness will surely follow.

Today in Japan, more and more mixed-race individuals are being chosen as national representatives in beauty pageants, and the entertainment industry is seeing a growing presence of mixed-race talents.

I, too, was honoured to become the first Black, mixed-race lead in a Japanese drama in 2023.

That didn't happen because the road was easy – it happened because I never gave up on expressing my true self.

Of course, there were countless hardships along the way.

But there is nothing for us to be ashamed of. We are human, just like everyone else.

In fact, perhaps we carry something even more special – a heart that can truly empathize with the pain of others.

Having mixed roots is not a weakness. It is a strength.

Before we can truly love others, we must first believe in ourselves, and love ourselves with all we've got.

And once we do, love for others will come naturally.

Ariana Miyamoto

Glossary

HERITAGE
The word 'heritage' brings together lots of special things that are relevant to your family's past – stories, traditions and values.

RACE
A system to identify and group people across the world based on the way they look, whether it's their skin colour, hair texture, facial features or eye shape.

RACIALIZED
The way people categorize or divide people into groups according to their race.

STEREOTYPE
A belief about a type of person or a group that is over simplified, not very thoughtful or considered, but nevertheless widely held and quite fixed in the minds of people.

ETHNICITY
A group of people who share the same heritage, background, traditions, customs and beliefs. Someone's ethnicity is different from their race, as it includes their society and culture.

IDENTITY
How you see who you are and how you fit into the world. This can be based on lots of things – including what you

look like, how you are racialized, your gender, ethnicity, your religious faith, dis/ability, languages you speak, where you grew up in the world, or where your parents were born.

MICROAGGRESSION
Microaggression is language or behaviour that can be intentionally or unintentionally unfriendly or negative in its attitudes towards groups who are already being treated as less important than others by society. We call this marginalization.

PREJUDICE
When someone makes a negative judgement about a person without getting to know them as an individual. People can have prejudices based on someone's gender, skin colour, wealth or where they're from.

DEMOGRAPHIC
A section or specific group of the population.

MULTICULTURALISM
When people from different backgrounds, with different skin colours, languages and traditions can all live together and share their unique ways of doing things.

SEGREGATION
the separation of different groups of people, maybe through different races, religions, or genders.

BLACK POWER
The Black Power group was made up of Black people

working together in the 1960s to stand up for their rights. It encouraged Black people to be proud of who they are, to stand up for their rights, and to have control over their own communities.

WHITE SUPREMACY
The belief that white people constitute a superior race and should therefore dominate society. This results in the exclusion of other racial and ethnic groups.

WINDRUSH
The Empire Windrush was a ship that came to Britain in 1948. People from Caribbean countries like Jamaica, Trinidad and Barbados came to help rebuild Britain after the Second World War.

PREROGATIVE
A power or right that only you have.

AFFIRMATION
Something positive you say to yourself as a reminder of something good or true about who you are, or who you want to be.

COLONIZATION
Foreign nations, who were generally white, took control of territories and land that were mainly inhabited by Black and Brown peoples. Subjugation, oppression and indoctrination around self-hatred and denigration of darker skin were all part of the control.

About the Illustrator

Tasia Graham is a multimedia illustrator based in London. She strives to create beautiful stories and environments where people can pause for a moment in tranquillity. She is interested in the spiritual, the space between time and imagination and likes to push her practice, creating scenic digital drawings which can be transformed into paintings, collage prints and immersive rooms.

Tasia is an introvert who loves daydreaming and watching clouds move. She likes to go on nature walks, dance... anything that gets her body moving. She lives in the city, for the fun and community, but her home will always be in the countryside or near a warm beach.

She was shortlisted for Penguin Student Design Awards 2021, emerging artist at JG Contemporary Gallery, and also featured on BBC Make it at Market show.

 # Acknowledgements

First I want to thank **all of you** – my readers. I am so excited by the idea that you have chosen to read this book and also by the thought that it may be in some way a help to you in feeling joyful or comfortable in your own expression of your identity.

My writing this book has been made possible by the incredible people who have generously shared their stories with me about being Mixed over the years. All of the insights I have gathered during the time I have been interviewing and talking to people about this subject have equipped me with a wealth of information that has helped me with not just this project but with others that touch on this subject. Thank you to everyone I've spoken with – from footballers to the chefs to the actors and actresses to the TV presenters and academics, to the incredible people with amazing life stories and anecdotes about identity, heritage and belonging.
I am honestly so thankful to all of you for trusting me to hear and care for your stories and I hope I have done you proud.

To C, to be believed in the way you believe in me – is something special. Thank you.

My dad, always constant, ever loving and supportive in every thing I do – you remain one of the greatest examples of what deep love and consistent care look like for me. You will never quite grasp how important crafting with pipe cleaners, stomping over rolling hills and Sunday movie sessions with you were for my powers of imagination.

My mum – there is too much to say so I'll keep it brief – you are the reason I am a writer and you always knew I was supposed to be one. Thank goodness you told me.

Nene – another important teacher in my life! The one who taught me the importance of passing on what you know, of holding on to the things that make you who you are and of sharing your love and your gifts with the rest of the world in your own way.

To the Mixed Heritage community that has been a great source of inspiration to me as we all work on our various projects bringing to light our many vastly different and similar narratives – a mention to just some of the people in this community whose work has been a comfort and whose camaraderie I have appreciated – Hanako Footman, Ela Lee, Afua Hirsch, Laxmi Hussain, Yuri Davis, Claire Finney, Melissa Legarda Alcantara, Maria P. Root, Anna Sulan, Farzana Nayani, Michelle Zauner, Trevor Noah, Emma Dabiri, Dr Melissa Wagner, Rosemary Adaser and so many others.

To my lovely pen pallers who contributed to this book: Dean Atta, Jassa Ahluwalia, Ashleigh Plumptre, India Amarteifio, Tori Tsui, Ryan Alexander Holmes, Asia Jackson, Fola Evans Akingbola, Ariana Miyamoto, Melissa Hemsley and Jessie Mei Li. Thank you for sharing your wisdom with us.

Thank you to Miss Hadaway who was the first teacher in my life to inspire creativity in me. I felt an immense sense of belonging in your primary school class and will never forget dancing in the rain outside the classroom as you frequently allowed us to do, nor learning to glaze a pot in the pottery kiln you used to bring into school. Thank you for encouraging my vivid imagination and my writing from such an early age.

To my literary agent Kirsty Milner at Stella Media – thanks for making sure this journey has been as seamless as possible and in general for being in my corner when it counts.

Cate Augustin – my editor at Macmillan – thank you for being so persistent in pursuing me to write this book, so gentle in your support and steadfast in your encouragement, especially when I was a little bit uncertain from my previous experience of writing a book. This book is important and I am so glad we have worked so hard on it together. Thank you for your help in shaping *Mixed* – I hope you're as proud of it as I am.

To the rest of my team at Macmillan – Ruth Redford, Clare Hall-Craggs, Cheyney Smith, Rachel Vale and Louisa Cusworth. Thank you for all the work you've done and will no doubt continue to do to help bring this book to life and get it into many hands.

Tasia Graham – thank you for your deliciously good illustrations – especially for the food related ones of which there are lots ☺ I really appreciate your style of course, but also your lovely note at the beginning of us working together to say how much you loved the book content.

To the friends who are ever-present cheerleaders in my life Sophie Clifford, Elise Funnell, Charmaine Murray, Bea Clarke, Sam Brown, Lisa Berry, Chantelle Wright, Holly Rebecca, Nerissa Pratt, Micaela Sharpe, Pip Jolley, Zeena Shah, Emma Jane Palin, Dounia Sghiri, Victoria Kasumu and Little Bex (Rebekah Kasumu) birthday twin, BEKA Prance and Alyssa Ordu.

To some of the children in my life whom I love dearly and who inspire me to write books like this: Ezra, Vivienne and Iyla.

A special note to my business co-founder, friend and all round favourite person to share a meme and a joke with – Mel – thank you for your help and advice on accurate cultural representation within this book. I'm so blessed to have you as a good friend and in so many other instances as a sage sounding board. ♡